For MARILYN -

A God We Can Believe In

A GOD WE CAN BELIEVE IN

Edited by
RICHARD AGLER
and RIFAT SONSINO

WIPF & STOCK · Eugene, Oregon

A GOD WE CAN BELIEVE IN

Wipf & Stock
An Imprint of Wipf and Stock Publishers
199 W. 8th Ave., Suite 3
Eugene, OR 97401

www.wipfandstock.com

PAPERBACK ISBN: 978-1-6667-3582-6
HARDCOVER ISBN: 978-1-6667-9336-9
EBOOK ISBN: 978-1-6667-9337-6

VERSION NUMBER 041122

Grateful acknowledgment is made to the following for permission to reprint previously published material:

The Jewish Publication Society for "TANAKH: The Holy Scriptures: The New JPS Translation According to the Traditional Hebrew Text." Philadelphia: 1988. (Some translations have been modified by the authors.)

Geoffrey A. Mitelman for elements of "Judaism, Science, and God" that have been adapted from his selected previous writings on sinaiandsynapses.org, as well as from the chapter "Science and Truth" in *These Truths We Hold*, forthcoming by HUC Press.

Simeon J. Maslin, for permission to reprint the chapter "What About Death?", previously self-published in *A God for Grown-Ups: A Jewish Perspective*, Xlibris, 2019.

For those who wish to believe

For those who no longer believe

For those who might again believe

אהיה אשר אהיה

Ehyeh asher Ehyeh

God will be what God will be.

God's Name, as revealed to Moses at the burning bush.

—Exodus 3:14

Contents

Preface
Why This Book?

IT IS SELF-EVIDENT THAT many of the characterizations of God found in our sacred texts, liturgies, and holidays are replete with images that large numbers of contemporary Jews find neither meaningful nor believable.

Our annual cycle is filled with references to a Deity who intervenes in history, supernaturally responds to prayers, protects his (sic) faithful and chosen, and executes righteous judgment. In the twenty-first century, such propositions engender doubt and disbelief in rabbis and laypersons alike. At the same time, they are a disincentive to Jewish engagement, commitment, and affiliation.

A God We Can Believe In is a response to this moment. Herein you will find contributions from leading rabbis and academics that articulate paths to Jewish hearts, minds, and souls with God-teachings that are spiritually compelling and intellectually sound.

Our authors present God in ways that are consistent with the facts that higher learning has established, the principles of reason, and their own life experiences. We are not speaking primarily to academics, but to all inquisitive Jews, and perhaps even non-Jews, who seek to live by these same lights.

The value and importance of the poetic, the metaphorical, and the ancient religious imagination are vital in Jewish tradition. At the same time, God-language, God-teaching, and God-understanding need to be coherent, comprehensible, and credible if modern Jews are going to hear it.

In these pages you will find a God that cannot be brushed aside by educated moderns; a God that does not violate the realities of logic or natural law; a God presented in accessible, yet deeply grounded, Jewish language; a God that can be lived with, and lived for.

Our hope is that this book will help secure a place for a living, non-mythical God at the heart of Jewish life in this generation and in generations to come. We endeavor to strengthen the connections between our people, our faith, and our tradition.

It is our further goal to impress upon our institutions the need to embrace new and systematic ways of addressing God in formal worship, of hearing God interpreted from the pulpit, of learning about God in classrooms, and of praying to God from future *siddurim*.

May our respective strengths strengthen us all—חזק, חזק, ונתחזק.

Lshalom,
Rabbi Richard Agler, DD
Rabbi Rifat Sonsino, PhD

Editors' Note

EACH OF OUR CONTRIBUTORS is recognized as a thought leader in their respective communities—and often beyond. We invite you to honor their wisdom as you ponder and consider their teachings and insights.

In addition to a passion for the subject, each author brings a distinctive personal style. Some write formally, some write conversationally, some write academically, and some write artistically. We trust you will find that this diversity of styles contributes to the overall richness of the volume.

Thank you for journeying with us in the search for *A God We Can Believe In*.

PART I

A BELIEVABLE GOD

God as the Energy of the Universe

—Rabbi Rifat Sonsino

OUR KNOWLEDGE, OURSELVES

For centuries, philosophers have been trying to find out how we know what we know. They have developed a series of theories to explain this puzzle, none of which answers all of our questions completely. I agree with the empiricists who posit that we know what we experience. However, limited human beings as we are, complete knowledge is beyond our comprehension or ability to grasp, collect, and record. The realization that our knowledge is limited has led me to concentrate on concepts and values in historical and religious texts that are open to interpretation. Now, these are things we can argue about!

When I wake up in the morning and realize that I am alive in a world operating in a reliable yet mysterious way, I express gratitude to God that has made me part of it. Rabbi Abraham J. Heschel (d. 1972) wrote, "Wonder or radical amazement is the chief characteristic of the religious man's attitude toward history and nature."[1] The awareness that the universe has an intricate composition has led many, including me, to revere life. Not only am I in awe of the workings of the world, but I am equally struck by the way our bodies operate harmoniously most of the time. I view human beings as bulks of energies stimulated by forces within and without. How does the heart know to beat regularly? How does our digestive system work so properly? The ancient rabbis, noting this wonder, even penned a prayer to be said upon waking up in the morning: "Blessed are You, God, Creator of

1. Heschel, *God in Search of Man*, 45.

3

the universe, who has formed the human body in wisdom, and has created in it intricate passages, vessels, and openings. It is clear to You that if one of them is blocked or opened, we could not stand before You. Blessed are You, God, who heals all flesh in a wondrous way."[2]

THE WORD "RELIGION"

What does the word "religion" mean? Some people derive it from the Latin *relegare,* meaning, to re-examine carefully. Others trace it from *religare,* which means to connect (with God). Even though the second is the most popular understanding of the word today, it is still vague. What does it mean to connect with God? The Hebrew language does not even have a dedicated word for "religion." In medieval times, we find the word *dat*—דת, which can mean law, custom, or faith. In modern Hebrew, a *dati*—דתי is a religiously observant person.

Of the various definitions of religion, I believe, Erich Fromm (d. 1980) provided the broadest one. He argued that religion gives the individual a "frame of orientation" as well as "an object of devotion."[3] Each of us has a frame of orientation through which we view the world and an object of devotion to which we pledge ultimate loyalty. I like that approach.

For me, religion needs to be defined broadly as a way to help us find our place in the world, with all of its limitations and possibilities. I agree with Rabbi Roland Gittelsohn (d. 1995), who defined it as "the study of the mutual spiritual relations between human organisms and their total environment."[4] As academic Dan Solomon states, "my religion is grounded in my understanding and experience of nature."[5] In this sense, I consider everyone religious because we all have the same concerns and expectations. Whether we are Jewish, Christian, Muslim, or other, the way that we respond to our personal existential questions becomes our religion. I think Judaism provides a sound interpretation of human life, and that is why, in addition to being part of the Jewish people, I choose to remain a religious Jew.

The term religion is much broader than observance. Observance deals with practices, religion refers to one's attitude to life in general. Also, even

2. Stern, *Gates of Prayer,* 51–52.

3. Fromm, *Psychoanalysis and Religion,* 21.

4. Gittelsohn, *Wings of the Morning,* 177.

5. Solomon, *A Jewish Perspective,* 271.

though most religious people are moral individuals, religion and morality are not one and the same. Many people claim to be religious while engaging in unethical behavior.

RELIGIOUS NATURALISM

Modern religious naturalism is a philosophical perspective that in general rejects the reality of the supernatural realm and finds religious meaning in the natural world. For most religious naturalists, our physical world is the center of our most significant experiences and understanding as discovered through scientific research. As humans are interconnected with one another, they all share a sense of reverence and awe toward the universe.

In the past, this view was promoted by people like Benedict Spinoza, Albert Einstein, George Santayana, and Samuel Alexander as well as Rabbis Mordecai Kaplan and Sherwin Wine. Stephen Hawking can be added as a modern proponent of this perspective.

GOD AS THE ENERGY OF THE UNIVERSE

One can conceive of God in a variety of ways. Historically speaking, the two major approaches are theism and non-theism. Most classical theists believe that:

a) God is one and alone.

b) God, though not possessing a body, is a spiritual being who expresses will, love, and concern for the created universe.

c) God is all-powerful, all-knowing, and all-good.

d) God is supernatural and trans-natural.

e) God knows us, hears our prayers, and answers them.

f) God rewards the faithful and punishes the wicked.

The existence of such a God is often argued in four different ways:

a) ontologically, namely, deriving God's existence from the idea of God;

b) teleologically, that is, deriving God's existence from the observed order of the universe, i.e., if there is an order, there must be an ordering mind;

c) cosmologically, deriving God's existence from the idea that God started motion without being moved;

d) using the moral argument that points to God as the source of all moral decisions.

One of the greatest obstacles to a theistically conceived God is the problem of good and evil. For if God is omnipotent and all-good, how does one explain, for example, the Holocaust? Is it because God could not impede the tragedy? That would make God less than all-powerful. Or, is it because God did not want to? That would make God less than loving and caring. It certainly cannot be that the Jews and others who died during this tragedy deserved their punishment! Nothing can justify this type of torture and mayhem. There must be another way to view God.

Jewish sages have promoted a variety of God concepts. There is Isaac Luria's mysticism (sixteenth century), Baruch Spinoza's pantheism (seventeenth century), Erich Fromm's humanism (twentieth century), and many others. I am more attracted to the views of the religious naturalists who consider God not as a "person" who relates to the universe as an Almighty human-like being, but more of a non-personal Mind or Energy that stands at the center of our existence. Thus, for example, Mordecai Kaplan (d. 1983) believed that God is the Power that makes for salvation and Roland Gittelsohn argued that God is the creative spiritual Seed of the universe. I maintain that many Jewish adults, young ones in particular, find this approach more appealing.

Based on observation and analysis, I see a certain order in the world around us and conclude that this implies the existence of an ordering Mind or an ordering power and energy that stands for God. I concur with Stephen Hawking who defines God as "the embodiment of the laws of nature,"[6] the manifestation of a universal energy that makes my existence possible. For this, I am very appreciative, and express my thanks to God through prayers of gratitude and works of loving-kindness that benefit my family and community. I affirm the freedom of the human will and live with the realization that I do not have all the answers for the tension that exists between good and evil, because I do not fully know all the inner workings of the universe. In the spirit of Spinoza, I also say that if we knew how the world operates, we could predict our next move. But alas, this is not within our ability. So, we live in an imperfect world and with limited abilities to understand the

6. Hawking, *Brief Answers*, 28.

mysteries around us, while desperately looking for meaning and purpose in our daily struggles.

WHAT PRAYER ACCOMPLISHES

Of the three major types of prayer (praise, gratitude, and petition), the prayers of petition create problems for many people. The reasons vary: we may expect an immediate answer that fails to materialize; the text of the prayer may be disconcerting because of its archaic nature, patriarchal language, or non-inclusive character; we may confuse nobility of expression with profundity of thought. In reality, the crux of the problem is theological. Heschel once said, "The issue of prayer is not prayer; the issue of prayer is God."[7] Consequently, if you believe, you can pray. For a long time I, too, subscribed to this notion. However, I eventually realized that people often struggle with prayer and theology at the same time. As theological views become clearer, prayers need to become more authentic. Prayer is a natural need of every human being. The question is what to expect from it? Here below are my conclusions:

a) To help create a good prayerful mood, one needs an inspiring text and uplifting music within an appropriate physical setting.

b) Prayers represent our hopes and expectations that should not be read as legal briefs but as poetry pointing to something higher.

c) One should refrain from praying for the impossible. God works through the laws of nature and is not likely to change the course of events no matter how fervent the prayer or pious the individual.

d) It is more important to express one's goals and aspirations through prayers than to expect an answer for them. If we are able to formulate our thoughts clearly and turn them into a program of action, the action itself becomes our answer.

e) Prayers do not change the world outside, but they give the worshipers an insight into themselves.

f) Even if at the moment it is not possible to enter into a prayerful mood, one can, and should, identify with the community as part of the worship experience. By praying together we can strengthen one another.

---

7. Heschel, *Man's Quest for God*, 58.

WHAT UNITES ALL JEWS?

I have often been asked: If you maintain that there are various definitions of God in Judaism, just as there are different paths of Jewish spirituality, what then binds us Jews—literalists and liberals—together? My answer is that we share the same history; we have the same tradition that is optimistic and this-world oriented; we cherish the same sacred books; we celebrate the same holidays and life-cycle events; we have a strong ethnic connection, and we welcome anyone who wants to share our life and fate. To be a Jew is a privilege, and we should be proud of it. I am also convinced that many sophisticated young Jewish adults around the world will be more attracted to a religious philosophy, such as the one I have proposed, one that is based on science, one that deals with real facts—not miracles and myths.

Rabbi Rifat Sonsino, Ph.D. is the Rabbi Emeritus at Temple Beth Shalom in Needham, MA, and a retired academic.

God and the Earth's Foundations

—Rabbi Ralph Mecklenburger

We begin with God's speech from the tempest near the end of the Book of Job in the *Tanakh*. Poor Job's children have been killed, his wealth destroyed, and now his health. He is convinced, by all appearances rightly, that he has done nothing to deserve such tragedy and suffering. He demands an explanation from the God who, by the standard piety of his time—and for many in our time—was believed to reward the righteous and reserve such awful suffering for sinners. Job's dogged insistence on an answer finally provokes a response from God. That answer reveals little about divine justice, but much about the state of human knowledge in the poet's time. God cows Job into silence with four chapters about Job's—and the readers'—ignorance. It begins:

> Who is this who darkens counsel,
> Speaking without knowledge?
> Gird your loins like a man;
> I will ask and you will inform Me.
> Where were you when I laid the earth's foundations?
> Speak if you have understanding. (Job 38:2–4)[1]

Rhetorical questions follow in magnificent poetry one after another, individually and collectively demonstrating God's awe-inspiring brilliance—and mortals' ignorance.

> Have you penetrated to the sources of the sea,

---

1. Biblical translations in this article are from *Tanakh* (Philadelphia: Jewish Publication Society, 1985), with the exception of the Isaiah quotation in the final paragraph, where *shalom* and *ra* have been translated by the author as "peace" and "evil" rather than the JPS "weal" and "woe" to highlight the echo in the *Siddur*, "peace" and "all."

Or walked in the recesses of the deep?
Have the gates of death been disclosed to you?
Have you seen the gates of deep darkness?
Have you surveyed the expanses of the earth?
If you know these—tell Me. (Job 38:16–18)

What about the weather—snow, hail, rain, dewdrops? (Job 38:22–30) And the constellations of the night sky? (Job 38:31–33) And the animals! Does the human "know the season when the mountain goats give birth? / Can you mark the time when the hinds calve?" (Job 39:1) Does Job know the secrets of the wild ox—and tame him for labor? (Job 39:9–12) What about the ostrich . . . horse, hawk, and eagle? (Job 39:13–30) Read on into chapter 40 for mythical beasts, fearsome to us but mere playthings for God!

The poetry is so dazzling that before reaching the mythical behemoth and Leviathan one might fail to notice that lots of what Job cannot even begin to explain, a panel of contemporary scientists—geologists, oceanographers, meteorologists, zoologists, etc., could explain or repudiate, perhaps while smiling indulgently at the charming mythical background. No, we were not there when the earth's foundations were laid, but science has taught us a great deal about how it happened, from Big Bang to the formation of stars and galaxies, and thus of our sun and earth, plus the wonders of biological evolution on the planet, and at which season mountain goats, hinds and other creatures give birth. In this age of science, moreover, our telescopes, microscopes, and other intricate devices have revealed to us aspects of reality not even imagined in antiquity—billions of galaxies and black holes, subatomic particles, and more: the nature of all being including ourselves and our electro-chemical thoughts. Compared to Job and his contemporaries, we know plenty.

But let's not get carried away here! As we learn more, we also discover how much more there is to know. I recently opened the newspaper and found a headline story on page one declaring that the Standard Model in physics might turn out to be significantly inaccurate, erroneous. At the Fermilab near Chicago the muon, a subatomic particle related to the electron, wobbled a bit passing through an intense magnetic field. "The result, physicists say, suggests that there are forms of matter and energy vital to the nature and evolution of the cosmos that are not yet known to science." One expert suggested that this may be a major step towards figuring out what dark matter, "25% of the universe by mass," is, and perhaps "why there is matter in the universe at all."[2]

For all our vaunted science, much remains mysterious to us. Still, a sophisticated contemporary Job might not be cowed so quickly and totally. The ancients came up with a seemingly reasonable response when they wondered where the world and its complexities originated: God created it! From their own experience, they knew cause and effect. So when effects of unknown cause were manifest they imagined hidden spirits, gods, and later, one God, made things the way they are. By modernity, enough had been learned that some religionists began to warn that a God who was the intellectual plug for the holes in our knowledge was becoming less and less needed.

God has had other functions, too, of course—judging "His" creatures and providing moral guidance, for instance. A widely shared faith can promote social cohesion and justify institutions (for better or worse, of course—monarchs and caste systems, too). But the "God of the gaps" was in danger of becoming the "incredible, shrinking God." Notably, when the COVID-19 pandemic swept the world even our most modern, technocratic societies were caught flat-footed. We did offer prayers and many found their spirits strengthened in the process. Few imagined God was punishing us—the biblical response when disaster struck or appeared imminent. We knew about viruses and inter-species transmission, after all. We did not imagine that mass repentance would save us, as it saved the Ninevites in the book of Jonah (3:5–10). That was all they knew to do. We closed our places of worship to limit contagion and poured millions of dollars into pharmaceutical research.

One might reasonably say that the search for treatment and cure was and is an act of faith. It is certainly possible, moreover, for a classic theist to insist that our prayers worked, that God led us to vaccines. But that is not what I or the people I know were thinking. This is the age of science. We look to religion, to *God*, not for explanations of how the world works or miraculous intervention, but for reassurance that there is purpose and logic, meaning, in a vast, impersonal universe. That, I believe, requires looking beyond personal God ideas (the Creator consciously running everything) to philosophical God ideas (a logic, system of laws, or force infusing creation with meaning). This is not a strictly modern move. Jewish philosophers such as Philo of Alexandria, Moses Maimonides, Benedict Spinoza,

2. Overbye, *New York Times*, April 8, 2021, A1, A19.

Hermann Cohen, and Mordecai Kaplan, to name a few of the better-known examples, presented God more abstractly, and compatible with what they regarded as the best thinking of their times.

The Job author was correct that no one fully understands God. Our philosophical tradition insists that all God-talk is metaphorical and approximate. So the personal God is supplemented even in the *Tanakh* with other metaphors: God as rock, as eagle, as fount of living waters (Ps 19:15; Exod 19:4; Jer 2:13). God need not only be pictured as king, father, or judge. Furthermore, the philosophers were consciously defending the idea of God against challenges from what they and their contemporaries regarded as the best thinking of their time.

In our time that means we need a God metaphor that fits the contemporary scientific ethos. So I propose thinking of God as the laws by which the universe operates. Picture God not as the conscious creator of the universe, but as the rules by which the universe came into being and continues to operate, the rules themselves—God a collective noun, the Order Itself—and not the author of the rules. A computer-age metaphor: think of God as the software which determines what the hardware does, a creative force or principle of organization unconsciously but manifestly shaping the possibilities for what is shaped. God, *for starters*, may be understood as the laws of science— physics, chemistry, biology, evolution, and more—and even some of the principles of morality![3]

"But wait!" some may say. "I want a God I can sense, love, feel somehow upheld by." Note the emphasis in the preceding paragraph on "for starters." Our relationship to the divine is more subtle and profound than the laws of science alone. When, many years ago now, I read philosopher Daniel Dennett's *Darwin's Dangerous Idea*, I was much taken with his assertion that the universe must operate the same way on Venus or Jupiter, or for that matter some distant galaxy, as it does here on earth in the Milky Way, an assertion which can be made even before we have traveled to those distant places because everything which exists developed from the moment of the Big Bang. Billions of years later the universe, trillions of miles across,

---

3. For some ethical principles as hard-wired in our brains, not known only from experience or revelation, see "Of Trolley Cars and Other Mind Games" and "Evolved Values" in Mecklenburger, *Our Religious Brains* (Woodstock, VT: Jewish Lights and Skylight Paths, 2012), 118–28, or Mecklenburger, *Why Call It God?: Theology for the Age of Science* (Eugene, OR: Wipf & Stock, 2020), 81–84.

is still expanding from that one speck. As Dennett put it, "There is only one Design Space, and everything actual in it is united with everything else."[4]

Thus we can use our scientific instruments to analyze the atmosphere on Mars or infer the composition of a distant star from the light it emits because it should all operate in accordance with the same laws (and if we find something that varies from that we will not think there are two natural orders, but will hypothesize, and test our theories, correcting the flaw in our thinking). I shared Dennett's concept—one design space—with my friend, Jewish Philosophy professor Neil Gillman of the Jewish Theological Seminary, some twenty years ago. Without skipping a beat, he responded, "Oh! You mean, '*Sh'ma Yisrael Adonai Eloheinu Adonai Ehad.*'" Most readers will recognize that as the basic affirmation of Jewish faith, "Hear, O Israel! The Lord is our God, the Lord alone." (Deut 6:4) Yes! If there is one God and not many, the universal order is one and consistent.

Now consider: the universal order is not only "out there" in the world and universe. We ourselves are products of that order. In a universe still developing after billions of years, we *homo sapiens* are late-comers who evolved only around 300,000 years ago. Our bodies are an incredibly complex part of creation, and the brain, the control center, as it were, with its hundred billion neurons, is the most complex mechanism on earth. The development of language to a degree way beyond the chirpings, grunts, and screams of other animals has facilitated our ability for abstract and systematic understanding, further opening the way for not only biological, but cultural, evolution.

As we have learned more and more about "the earth's foundations" and now the neurology of our own thinking, an appreciation for the laws of science should be one element of modern theology. We cannot send our children off to the best schools to learn how the world works and then expect them to believe in miracles and mythic history. But we and they can surely appreciate, even love, the lessons to be learned from human culture generally, and our own people's Torah, the "tree of life" which has grown from it: our literature, history, values, and sense of the holy.

All human cultures appreciate and promote intangible realities that lend meaning to our lives. We find meaning in phenomena that most of us are convinced are real, though philosophers and other experts in each field

4. Dennett, *Darwin's Dangerous Idea*, 135. For applying this beyond Darwinian evolution and back all the way to the Big Bang, see my correspondence with Dennett in *Why Call It God?*, 27.

cannot even fully agree on their definitions. I cannot provide a complete list of what I like to call "divine intangibles," but it should certainly include justice, love, peace, truth, beauty, courage, compassion, and morality.

Such value-laden terms express our rational judgment *and* our emotional reaction to experience. The gorgeous painting, the loving person, the heroic deed, the just outcome, and so on, are genuine facets of the world's order and our experience. "Wow" moments, spiritual highs, the times when we sense that life is a grand gift, are the quintessential religious moments demonstrating to each of us that the world can feel holy and we are blessed to be alive. These are the moments when the order inside us recognizes the positive aspects of the order outside us.

The order within and the order of all are one and the same. Sensing that, we like to speak of a spark of God in each of us, borrowing the metaphor from medieval mystics. Can science as well as theology study this? Of course. While science strives to be strictly rational and analytic, in religion we can welcome the emotional, too, all of it realized by our physical brains. Religion is not a reaction to the supernatural which is myth, but to the order of existence both inside and outside us. If God is understood as the scientific order of which moderns are convinced, and the intangible blessings we each experience, there are no atheists. God understood this way is the perceived reality of our lives.

Suddenly this more philosophical God-talk is not so coldly rational—but not irrational, either! The divine intangibles are the things we live for, and which give us a sense of life's meaningfulness. At births and marriages, even funerals, or looking out at grand vistas or discovering the finest in the arts, or extraordinary athletic performances, or historic achievements, or . . . whatever fills *you* with gratitude for life, the world, and relationships, we know we are blessed to be alive. We can have that, moreover, without believing in miracles or otherwise suspending our intellects.

What about the ugly and false, the cruel and evil? There is only one reality. As discussed above, we mostly find life a blessing, but the divine order is not there strictly for our benefit. Though our deeds have an impact on the world, we are not its masters, but are subject to its order. We naturally think of the good things as we look for evidence of goodness and meaning in life and history. But Jewish thought follows Isaiah, who presented God saying, "I form light and create darkness; I make peace and create evil; I the Lord do all these things." (Isa 45:7) We echo this in our prayer book every morning, praising God as "creator of light and darkness, maker of peace and creator of all." We need not pretend that evil is an illusion, like Job's "friends" who kept trying to convince him he had sinned and must deserve his suffering. Life has its painful and tragic elements and no one escapes wholly unscathed. But God as abstract principle does not *knowingly* inflict pain or injustice. Despite the negatives, most agree that life is a grand journey and that we, the conscious products of the universal order, can add to the store of divine intangibles, working towards a better world for tomorrow.

———————

Rabbi Ralph Mecklenburger is Rabbi Emeritus at Beth-El Congregation in Fort Worth, Texas, and author of, *Our Religious Brains* and *Why Call It God?: Theology for the Age of Science.*

Can a Child be a Religious Naturalist?

—Rabbi Sandy Eisenberg Sasso

Our children hear God talk all around them, whether within their own families and congregations, in public discourse, or among their friends. Most of the theology they encounter lacks nuance and imagination. Many adults, unclear of their own beliefs, assume that children are unsophisticated when it comes to theology, incapable of engaging abstract ideas. Assuming that they lack the philosophical ability, religious educators dismiss their questions or avoid addressing them seriously.

Children are told what God can do to them if they are bad or for them if they are good, but not what they can do because of God. As children get older and their early notions of God are challenged by their own experiences and developing intellectual sophistication, their theological curiosity turns to indifference or resentment. They question themselves when their prayers are not "good enough" to heal a loved one. They are angry when their sense of fairness is betrayed and when they feel cheated. Suggesting that some things are beyond human understanding and offering notions such as rewards in a world to come are inadequate. On the one hand, supernaturalist and exclusionary theologies have the potential to foster dangerous notions about what it means to be a person of faith; on the other hand, they lead to the rejection of belief in God as a childish fantasy.

As children grow into adulthood, the simplistic notions of God as a Cosmic Puppeteer or Celestial Bellhop are often dismissed along with the Tooth Fairy, and nothing remains to take their place. The images of the Divine as a graying and bearded grandfather or crowned and majestic King prove inadequate.

A naturalist understanding of God is not only "naturally" accessible to children, but an important component of their growing spiritual lives. When we say that God is a process, at work within the universe, between us, instead of above us, empowering us, instead of having power over us, we are suggesting a different way of imagining the divine. Instead of a transcendent celestial being, God is in our capacity to transcend ourselves and grow in relationship to others.

Children are aware of their ever-changing bodies, even as they recognize their identity as stable. Their being has a permanence, even as their "self" continues to evolve. So, they can be taught of a God who changes in relationship to the world and time, yet whose divinity remains a constant. As children are their physical bodies, but also transcend them, so God is in the world and more than that. God can be understood as the reality that gives us courage in the midst of fear, graciousness in the presence of difficulty, hope at the heart of doubt, the life force that brings us joy and teaches us gratitude.

We communicate this to children by the ways in which we talk with them about God. When those who most frequently speak of the divine suggest that natural disasters are acts of God, or tragic events are God's will, children learn supernaturalism. The only alternative they come to know is atheism or secularism. Religious naturalism can communicate a different language, and the earlier we speak it, the more likely and more quickly it will be learned. It should not be delayed, so that it becomes a foreign language, harder to acquire and understand.

The most helpful God-language is rich in metaphor, connected to concrete situations, and open to a continuing conversation. Tangible experience, compelling narrative, and metaphoric language are windows to the divine. Children attribute animacy to all of nature. Trees talk, flowers dance, and grass sings. Nature is their playground, and play is the way that they make meaning of their world. Can religious naturalists imagine ritual as "godly play,"[1] a set of traditional "tools" created long before we were born that help ground us, connect us, carry us through joy and sorrow, and provide the foundation for reinterpretation and transformation?

Even though we warn against depicting God in anthropomorphic terms, we nonetheless recognize the need to clothe the divine in human garb. God is not lessened by the splendor of metaphor that arises out of

1. "Godly Play" is a term coined by Dr. Jerome Berryman for a method of religious education.

encounters. The problem isn't that there are any images at all, but that there are too few of them, and almost none that relate to a child's experiences. What resonance do Shepherd and King have for those who live in a democracy and an urban/suburban environment? The fewer images offered, the more we stifle a child's rich imagination, restrict God, and risk idolatry, allowing one image to be the absolute and perfect one. The more metaphors, the less likely any one image will be taken literally. In fact, the more we come to know, the closer we come to understanding the vastness of the divine. As we are in the process of becoming older, so God is in the process of growing with us.

To that end, I have dedicated my career as a children's book author. I have wanted to help children appreciate both a more accessible and more nuanced understanding of God. *In God's Name* is a story written to that purpose. In it, people call God by different names, depending on their unique experiences. A farmer calls God "Creator of Life," a young woman cradling a child calls God "Mother," and a child who is lonely calls God "Friend." Each person claims the name he/she has for God is the right name, better than anyone else's. Then they all come together and call out their names for God at the same time. They realize that all the names for God are good, that no name is better than another, and they call God "One."

After reading this story, I ask children, what is their favorite name for God? They most frequently select Mother or Friend. Sadly, no one had ever given them permission to do that. They had been educated to parrot back names that meant little to them or that they did not understand. Appreciating the many ways in which God is experienced, helps children recognize that the divine changes, yet is ever-present in their lives in different ways at different times. God, who can be Healer, Redeemer, Mother, Father, Friend is not a physical entity but a relational presence manifest in the natural world and through encounters with others.

By inviting youngsters to discover metaphors for God, we nurture their imagination and understanding of a God big enough to include all, especially their own experience. If God can be like the ocean, and a child the wave, as one youngster shared with me, and God can be a trampoline who helps a person bounce back when he has fallen down, as another young man suggested, then the divine remains a pulsating presence throughout life, alive in the world, not out of and apart from it.

Through a series of vignettes, *God's Paintbrush*, my first children's book, invites children to experience the divine in their everyday experiences from such ordinary events as a friend's moving away to a child's getting lost, from learning to ride a bike to crossing a street. Each vignette ends with a question that suggests ways in which the readers can make God's presence active in their own lives. Think of God as electricity. It exists in potential in the electrical wires but is only manifested through turning on the switch, that is through human activity. The questions ask children how they will turn on the switch. The book is not meant to tell children what to believe, because no one can really do that for another. Its goal is to help them sense the divine presence in their lives and to open up an ongoing conversation between and among children, their parents, and teachers.

In one of the book's vignettes, a group of children go on a hike and learn what an echo is. The question that concludes the scenario is, How are you like God's echo? One child responded, "You know, an echo does not have to be a sound." Questions like, "What makes you feel big enough to do something all by yourself, for the very first time?" suggest that God is not a Being but a Process, a reality within and without us that helps us grow, create, and heal the world.

As religious naturalists, how might we explain death to children? What would it mean to talk about heaven in a naturalistic rather than other-worldly way? In *For Heaven's Sake*, I suggest that heaven does not have to be an ethereal, physically habitable place up there, above and beyond any reality we know. After the death of his grandfather, a young boy accompanies his grandmother to all those places his grandfather loved and served others. His grandfather's presence is still felt by the people who knew him, and the boy comes to understand how actions leave lasting impacts that continue through time. Eternal life takes on a new meaning, and the story gives him the language to express it. His grandmother explains, " . . . We can get close to heaven and to God in a place in our hearts. I feel there is a part of Grandpa in all the places and people we visited today, and a little bit of heaven, too."

Most religious education teaches about prayers, but not how to pray. Religious naturalism offers the possibility of modeling prayer that is a way to name your greatest joy, your deepest sorrow, your most profound fear, to express your sincerest need, alone or in community, without expecting magical rewards. It is a way to look at who you are in the process of becoming. It provides a new vocabulary for speaking about God and prayer that becomes an expression of hope, belonging, and awe.

Children deserve our honesty. As religious naturalists, we are remiss in postponing God conversations until adulthood. Blessed with a deep sense of wonder, a relentless curiosity, and delightful spontaneity, children are ready for deeper discussions about the divine. They appreciate the holy in the natural world, within themselves, and in their encounters with others. When we name our experiences of surprise and beauty, gentleness and compassion, fear and courage, justice and kindness as sacred, and encourage children to do the same, we begin to provide a new religious language. When we ask and invite questions, we teach that belief is an ongoing process that is not afraid of doubt. When we speak of a belief that is intellectually engaging, ethically compelling, and spiritually uplifting, we provide an antidote to cynicism and despair. When we reimagine what the word "holy" means, we see the world not as something to be manipulated but to be sanctified. We can acknowledge what children share with us, even as we open up one another to new ways of thinking and develop a fresh vocabulary of faith.

The conversation that this essay opens up for children should engage us as adults as well. Our role is not merely to mentor children in their understanding and experience of the sacred, but to walk humbly with them on their journey.

Religion begins with experience and is then captured in story. That story is concretized and recalled through ritual. Only then is it reflected in theology and philosophy. The philosophy of religious naturalism is grounded in a way of experiencing reality that can be shared with children through symbol, ritual, and story.

The prophet Isaiah says, "All of Your children (*banayikh*—בניך) shall be taught of God and great shall be the peace of You children." (Isa 54:13) The Talmud adds, "Read not Your children, (*banayikh*), but rather Your builders, (*bonaiyikh*—בוניך).[2] Children require reliable building blocks to which they are invited to add their own mortar and bricks to construct their edifice of faith.

Dr. Sandy Eisenberg Sasso is Rabbi Emerita of Congregation Beth-El Zedeck in Indianapolis, Indiana, and Director of the Religion, Spirituality, and the Arts Initiative at IUPUI Arts and Humanities Institute. She is

2. b. Ber 64a.

the author of over twenty-five nationally and internationally acclaimed children's books and two books for adults including, *Midrash—Reading the Bible with Question Marks.*

Reverent Agnosticism

What to Believe and What Not to Believe about God

—RABBI HILLEL COHN

BEHAVING, BELONGING . . .

THERE ARE THREE MAJOR categories of Jewish belief: God, Torah, and Israel, categories that were first perhaps mentioned in that great mystical work, the Zohar, where it is said, "The Holy One, blessed be He, the Torah, and Israel are one."[1] In a sense, those three, God, Torah, and Israel, are our Jewish Trinity.

But there is another Trinity, one of relatively more recent vintage. It has been said that the Jewish experience is essentially one of "Belonging, Behaving and Believing." The order of those words is interchangeable and there is no suggestion that one is of greater importance than the other. Yet for many, it is the Jewish experience of Behaving that has been the most defining. Behaving takes two forms: engaging in ritual or ceremonial acts and putting the teachings of Jewish tradition to work day-to-day, i.e., living ethical and moral lives.

Belonging, though, is also important. Rabbi Mordecai Kaplan wrote, ". . . Contrary to the usual assumption, in the normal experience of Jewish life, belonging takes precedence over believing, in the same way as feeding a hungry man takes precedence over reading poetry to him."[2]

---

1. *Zohar, Aharei* 73a.
2. Kaplan, *Questions Jews Ask,* 5.

For good reason, we emphasize Behaving and Belonging and, for the most part, are more reticent to concern ourselves with Believing. The old adage of "I really don't care what you believe as long as you behave properly" is one that most, if not all of Jews, seem to live by.

BELIEVING

But there comes a time when Believing IS significant.

What are we supposed to believe about God? While there is never a real test of belief imposed on Jews as there might be in Christianity—not even when a youngster becomes a *Bar Mitzvah* or *Bat Mitzvah*—there is an implied assumption that we are a believing people and that we share a common faith. But the fact is that we don't.

One of the best sources for knowing what we might be assumed to believe is found in the People's text, i.e., the *Siddur,* the Jewish prayer book. The *Siddur* assumes that we believe certain things about God. What are some of those things?

The service for the Eve of *Shabbat* provides some examples. In both traditional and liberal versions, God is referred to as Lord and Maker. A psalm that is part of the *Erev Shabbat* liturgy acclaims God as the Rock of Our Salvation, and King. Another proclaims, "*Adonai* made the heavens [and] rules the world justly and in faithfulness." Ps 99 expresses the belief that God is Mighty. In Ps 92, God is lauded for acting with lovingkindness every morning and with faithfulness every night.

The *siddur* goes on to proclaim that God is praiseworthy, creator of a universe which for the most part is dependable and orderly, Revealer of Torah, and the Lover of Israel, the Jewish People. The *Sh'ma* proclaims that God is *Ehad*, One. God is praised for having redeemed the Jewish People, the Israelite community, from slavery. Another prayer concludes with the belief that God is the God who "spreads the tabernacle of peace over us, over Israel, and over Jerusalem."

The central prayers of *Erev Shabbat* ascribe even more qualities to God. Those prayers assume that Jews believe fully in those attributes of God. God is the One who upholds the falling, heals the sick. And the rest of the central prayer of the service, the *tefilah,* adds to the list of God-beliefs such things as listening to prayer and making peace—if not for all of the human community then minimally for the people of Israel.

That's just what Jews are assumed to believe about God in the service for the eve of *Shabbat,* one of the briefer services. Think of the many other things that could be extracted from the *Siddur* for weekdays, for *Shabbat* morning, for festivals, or from the *Mahzor* for the High Holy Days.

NON-BELIEVING

There are many things to believe about God. But there are also things not to believe.

The late Rabbi William Silverman wrote, "If man is to seek and find the help that comes from God, he must have the courage to eradicate outmoded superstitions and archaic stereotypes of divinity and advance from a kindergarten-concept of deity to a mature consideration of a supreme and spiritual being."[3]

He goes on to say, "It is imperative that religious fantasies, whimsical delusions, and childlike stereotypes of God be dissipated. The false and transitory euphoria induced by the happiness pills of respectable religion will not satisfy those who cannot accept the belief in the Lord as a Man of War, or of God as a divine superman and heavenly magician."[4]

While there are many volumes that seek to explain and promote traditional beliefs in God, an especially fine book of Jewish theology is a slim volume that was intended to be a textbook for young Jewish children in first or second grade. Its author was Dorothy Kripke. In *Let's Talk About Being Jewish,* each one or two-page chapter begins with a poem, many of which were subsequently turned into songs. The book was intended to help children but it can just as well be of immense help to adults. Here are just a few of her short theological lessons:

> "God is not a person,
> Or moon, or stars, or sun.
> God is the good that's in the world.
> And God is only One."[5]
> "God is never seen,
> And yet we know God's there,
> Because we see the things God does

3. Silverman, *Religion for Skeptics,* 22.

4. Silverman, *Religion for Skeptics,* 32.

5. Kripke, *Let's Talk,* 8,12, 68.

And feel God's loving care."[6]
"If we love God, then we should love
God's children everywhere.
The Bible therefore teaches us:
Be loving and be fair."[7]

In writing for Jewish youths years ago, Rabbi Roland Gittelsohn said that "It would be incorrect, however, to assume that Judaism places no restrictions on our thinking about God. One cannot pretend that faith in Jesus as the Messiah is a Jewish belief, or that the [Christian] Trinity is an acceptable Jewish doctrine, or that worship of the sun can be included within Judaism."[8] He wrote that for a view of God to be legitimately Jewish it must affirm that "God is One—one in quantity and unique in quality. . . that God is spiritual, not physical . . . and that God demands ethical behavior of those who believe in Him . . . [Judaism] assumes that God exists, then hastens to ask what we must do, how we must act in order to demonstrate our faith in God."[9]

A way to believe in God that makes sense was articulated by Rabbi Harold Schulweis. He suggests that we think of God not as subject but as predicate. "Not the qualities of divinity but the divinity of the qualities is essential to belief. To illustrate this inversion, I turn to the liturgical life and specifically to the translation of benedictions. How are the blessings of the prayer book to be understood in accordance with the idea of Godliness? One of the first blessings we learn is the benediction over bread: 'Blessed are thou O Lord our God. Ruler of the universe, who brings forth bread from the earth.' With the idea of Godliness, our attention is directed not to the noun but to the activity that brings forth bread from the earth. What are the events that bring this bread to the table?"[10]

Arriving at our own answers begins when we discard things that we can't, in good conscience or reasonably, believe about God.

If there is one term that might well describe the Jewish concept of God, it is "Reverent Agnosticism." What that means is that we acknowledge that there is much about God that we do not know nor will ever know. We DO know how belief in God functioned for people in times past. And we

---

6. Kripke, *Let's Talk*, 12.

7. Kripke, *Let's Talk*, 68.

8. Gittelsohn, *A Jewish View*, 3.

9. Gittelsohn, *A Jewish View*, 4.

10. Harold Schulweis, *For Those Who Can't Believe*, 133.

DO know how it functions for us today. But to assert that we know the true nature of God is arrogant. It is a mark of maturity to be an agnostic, one who freely and proudly says, "I do not know," and at the same time treats the word God with the utmost of reverence in recognition of all that it has meant for people through the ages. God is not a word to be used casually. It is a word to be used with the utmost reverence. As the word or idea that brings together those things that make for true human salvation, it is a word that ought to evoke from us the highest response. And that response is to disavow the numerous unreasonable, irrational qualities attributed to God and instead seek to become more godly, and God-like.

Hillel Cohn (HUC 1963) served as rabbi of Congregation Emanu El of San Bernardino, CA from 1963–2001 and is now Rabbi Emeritus of the congregation. He earned a Doctor of Ministry degree from Claremont School of Theology.

The Faith of a Skeptic

—Rabbi Bruce S. Block

A Litvak is a natural-born skeptic. I am a Litvak. That is my heritage. Both my grandfathers were born in Lithuania and emigrated to the United States. Not sure about my grandmothers, but one of them may also have been a Litvak.

Other European Jews stereotyped Litvaks as being rational, unemotional, critical. Litvaks were thought of as being people whose commitment to Judaism was purely intellectual, and who were by nature, skeptical, and thereby, possibly prone to heresy.

So, you see, I am by nature, a skeptic. But I also have always been curious, open to exploring ideas and experiences. Not without a rational, critical eye to these ideas and experiences, though.

God. What do I think about God? What is my experience of God, if any? Stories. Do you mind a few stories? Anecdotes, really. You see, we Jews are a story-telling people.

Carl was a member of a congregation I led years ago. He was a professional engineer. He was always rather serious and often very focused. He served on the Temple board and loved chairing the committee which oversaw buildings and grounds. Anything mechanical that needed attention or fixing was right up his alley. One year, we had a one-day board retreat. At the retreat, there was a session on God. During that session, quite unexpectedly, Carl broke down sobbing. "I've searched for God. I've tried to find God. I've tried so hard. And I can't find God."

Carl is like so many of us. We search for God. We try to find God. And we can't find God. Believe? How can we believe in something so elusive? Like Carl, and perhaps like you, I had periods in my life where I searched for

God. After all these years, how I wish I could sit down with Carl and have a conversation. I'd like to ask him what kind of God he was searching for, what paths he had taken on his search, and what he was expecting to find. I'd like to tell him of my own search and where it led, how my path took me through our tradition, the writings of many philosophers and theologians of various times and places, and how science and reason played a role.

Mordechai is an old friend. He was ordained a rabbi in the Chabad-Lubavitch movement. We used to study Jewish texts together once a week. And, of course, we would talk. Aware of our differences, we were also respectful of them. He once told me that not a leaf falls from a tree without *Ha-Shem* having willed it. *Ha-Shem*: Hebrew for The Name. It is the term many, if not most, Orthodox Jews use when referring to God. The notion of God is so filled with awe and reverence, and not a little fear and trembling, too. So, a special term is used, lest one diminish that awe and fear and reverence.

Someone once asked me, "What is the difference between you and Mordechai?" The difference? Mordechai and God have a relationship. God is real and the relationship is personal. For me, God is a concept, rooted much more in science and philosophy, two subjects I approached with reason and critical thinking. That is how I was taught at university. That is also how I was taught at my rabbinical seminary. A Litvak is made for such teaching.

I found the God Mordechai believes in to be difficult for me to accept. I could not find evidence to support his belief that not a leaf falls from a tree without *Ha-Shem* willing it. Too much exposure to botany. And, what if a branch fell from that tree, injuring, or worse, killing someone? Did *Ha-Shem* will that, too?

So, what do I make of God? There is a mystery at the heart of the universe. Does it have an origin? What about the planet on which we live? How was it created, shaped, and formed? How did all the plants and animals, and we humans, come to be? Is there some larger purpose and meaning to our lives? Why do we have to die? And what, if anything, happens to us after we die? Science pushes away as much of the mystery as it can, given the limited abilities of the most brilliant of scientists. But the unknown parts of these eternal, and possibly unanswerable, questions gnaw away at us in our existential curiosity. Religion emerges in an effort to answer some of these existential questions. It is one response to them. And it posits God at the heart of the mystery.

I studied great thinkers, philosophers, and theologians. I looked at arguments for the existence of God (cosmological, ontological, teleological, etc.), and considered notions like panentheism and religious naturalism. The result is that the term God has meaning for me. But it does not mean what it means to Mordechai, nor do I think it is the God for whom Carl searched. God, for me, is the mysterious power that enables this universe to exist and operate by the laws of nature described to me in the sciences I have studied.

So, what is Torah? I am a part of a particular people for whom Torah records their quest for God, and their experience of God and each other along the way. It contains wisdom regarding how to live life together with others in such a way as to enhance both physical and spiritual survival. Many of its stories are not literally true. Yet, like all stories, they do contain truth.

Prayer? Does the God I believe in answer prayer? No. But I answer to prayer. Prayer is a way of focusing on the core values my Jewish heritage has taught and in which I believe. It strengthens me in my resolve to live by them. If I arise from prayer unchanged, then my prayers have not been answered, But, if I arise from prayer changed, strengthened, inspired, then my prayers have been answered.

And what happens to us after we die? Another story. Two brothers asked me to give a brief lecture on Jewish views of the afterlife in their mother's memory at her funeral. One was a retired professor at an Ivy League university; the other was a concert pianist. They said that, since I didn't know their mother, and since one of them would speak about her, and since she, a European-born intellectual, was not a believer, that would be a way to honor her memory. So, here are some excerpts from my brief lecture in memory of their mother.

"Any religion seeks to respond to the fact that we human beings live our lives between the two termini of birth and death by trying to answer the question of what happens to us after we die. Almost any answer which has been posited by the world's great religions, east and west, can be found expressed in a Jewish way at various points along the Jewish historical continuum."

"A Reform notion prevalent in the latter part of the twentieth century was that immortality could be attained in three different ways. First, in the genetic sense. Those who have offspring have some continuation of their being in the DNA they have contributed to their children and grandchildren. Second, there is the sphere of remembrance. We continue on in the memory of the living who knew us, and who called us to mind. And, third, some have left a lasting contribution to humanity in artistic creations, scientific achievements, or significant actions which are remembered long after they are gone, by people who never knew them, whose minds interact with the creations of their minds."

"So much of Jewish thought about life and death, the soul and immortality, has had the intent of giving us comfort and hope, and, I might add, sometimes providing extrinsic motivation for ethical behavior. But, in our age, we cannot know for certain what happens to us after we die. We can only offer comfort to the living, and hope that we are remembered for blessing."

Indeed, it would be comforting to think that I might continue on in some way after I die. But I can't think of any other way that is consistent with rational thought than what I had expressed in those words I spoke those few years ago.

Faith and reason: are they antagonistic or complementary? That is a question with which many have struggled over the centuries. The late Milton Steinberg, a noted rabbi and thinker of the twentieth century, chose to work through this question in a novel he wrote about a first-century Talmudic sage who became a heretic. By fleshing out what few details are known about him, Steinberg imagined the life of that Sage, Elisha ben Abuya. The book, *As a Driven Leaf*, focuses on the conflict between faith and reason. This is a theme with which the philosophically trained Steinberg struggled in his own spiritual life in his effort to frame a systematic Jewish theology. He sought a way to reconcile, or at least accommodate, and perhaps even harmonize, the contrast. I think that writing *As a Driven Leaf* was part of that process, both spiritually and intellectually. Moreover, I think it was a way for him to communicate with an audience beyond his congregation at the Park Avenue Synagogue, who might also be struggling both intellectually and spiritually with the conflict. Modern Jews, to be sure, but perhaps others, as well.

Steinberg believed that Jewish religious observance must rest on thought about the nature and purposes of God. In the last of four lectures delivered shortly before his death, he concluded that, "Religion is more than theology. . . The enterprise of faith is [not one] of reason alone or of faith alone." He had already been working through that notion in *As a Driven Leaf*. At the end of his novel he depicts Elisha ben Abuya as telling his pupil, Rabbi Meir, that while reason and faith have both failed him, he confesses that he has learned that faith and reason are not antagonists.

Jews of past ages regarded Elisha ben Abuya as more than a heretic. To them, he was an apostate. A heretic differs with the dogma of a particular faith. An apostate rejects that faith entirely. As punishment for his apostasy, the Talmud erases his name, referring to him as *Aher*, meaning "the other" in passages referencing him. But I think had Elisha lived in our era he might have found a theological home in Reform Judaism. He would have found its openness to theological search and questioning to be quite compatible.

So, what about me? Am I a heretic? To an Orthodox Jew, most likely. To the most extreme branches of Jewish Orthodoxy, the *Haredim*—often referred to as ultra-Orthodox, I might even be considered an apostate. But just consider me a skeptic, true to my Litvak roots—open to questions, looking critically and analytically at answers, valuing reason, appreciating all learning, both from our tradition and from secular studies, and committed to a Judaism that is both intellectually satisfying and spiritually fulfilling.

I would like to imagine that there is a God who knows me and who cares about me. That would be a comforting thought. And there have been those moments, I must admit. But in the end, in my most rational and skeptical innermost Litvak, I am comfortable with a universe that is mysterious; its very existence—and mine, too—enabled by a power far beyond my understanding. That power is what I call God. And that power inspires in me both awe and humility.

Rabbi Bruce S. Block, DMin, DD is the Rabbi Emeritus of Temple Sinai of Bergen County, Tenafly, NJ

God of the Drunks

—Rabbi Andrea C.

Funny, he didn't look like a rabbi. He looked really normal. Like all of us. Just another recovering drunk, sitting in a room with me. But I'd heard there was a rabbi in AA. And as the only other Jewish person in AA (so it seemed), I was seeking out someone who I believed would understand my struggle to find God, better than anyone else.

You see, it was never my intention to become an alcoholic. Raised as a "nice Jewish girl" in Westchester County, New York, it was understood that my trajectory would include going to college, meeting a nice man, having a family, and upon reaching retirement, move to Florida. So when I found myself at twenty years old, unable to fulfill this plan because I was losing the battle with the disease of alcoholism, I checked myself into a thirty-day drug and alcohol rehabilitation program at a Catholic Hospital in upstate New York.

During that time, my parents were mortified that one of their children was an alcoholic. What would their friends and neighbors say if they knew? Riddled with shame, they did what they thought was best, which was to disown me.

After I finished rehab, I had nowhere to live—no place to go that seemed friendly. I went on welfare and ended up in a halfway house. This was certainly not how I was supposed to end up in life.

I had been going to Hebrew school since the age of seven. During that time, I received the best of what Conservative Judaism had to offer: a great education, Jewish summer camp, Hebrew high school. I was there for all of it. And yet, in all of that time, no one ever asked me about my belief in or my conception of God. And thus, while I had the belief that God existed, I couldn't articulate my own position on the matter. Certainly, I could concede there was a God, but if that were really the case, God hadn't done too much for me lately.

So I thought.

And then I became active in Alcoholics Anonymous. Although AA is not a religious program, it does have a spiritual component. Basically, AA urges the member to find a power greater than oneself to believe in. Because let's face it, for many struggling alcoholics, alcohol is a power greater than ourselves. We believed in the power of alcohol. It worked for many of us and enabled us to do things we wouldn't normally be able to do: ask someone on a date, dance without embarrassment, go to school or work, even just be around our loved ones. These are things normal people do without alcohol on any given day. But for a real alcoholic who depends on alcohol to be able to function, it is truly a crutch.

The first few months of sobriety were difficult, to say the least. I was actively going to Alcoholics Anonymous meetings. I was listening to the others at the meeting speak about their conception of their Higher Power. But, I didn't believe I could believe in their concept of God. It was either too New Testament based, or too New Agey. I wasn't crazy about the idea of believing in a God that only loved me conditionally. I also wasn't excited about a God that would want me to get into a yoga pose on a daily basis and forsake all possessions.

The elders of the AA group explained to me that I had the God thing all wrong. Alcoholics Anonymous doesn't ask us to take on someone else's God concept. It asks us to come up with a conception that works for us.

So, I didn't have to believe in anything that didn't fit me. I just had to come up with what I believed in.

The problem was, at twenty years old, I had nowhere to turn. It had been years since I had graced the doors of a synagogue. The internet hadn't been invented yet, so there was no easy place to research. As fate would have it, a few days later, I sought out someone who was to revolutionize how I saw God. I had heard that there was a Reform rabbi who had been in AA for a few years. I'm not sure what I was expecting when I saw him. Maybe I was shocked at how, well, normal he seemed. After the meeting, I went and asked if he'd be willing to meet with me, and we made an appointment.

When I sat with him in his office, I explained my predicament. I needed to find a God that would help me recover from this disease. But I didn't know how to access that God. I tried finding God in the Torah. The God of

Torah was sometimes vengeful, jealous, and conditional. God seemed scary and although quite powerful, I didn't see how this God could intervene and actually help me, a drunk, have any kind of a chance at rebuilding my life. And yet, all over AA, I heard stories of people putting their lives back together, a day at a time. I was skeptical but curious. Could this rabbi help me find this power?

The rabbi suggested, "Why not believe in God as 'Good Orderly Direction' that you get from the 'Group Of Drunks?'" So instead of approaching God as a deity, I could receive God's direction from the guidance of the AA group. This was a revolutionary concept to me at the time. I no longer had to try to pray to a deity I couldn't seem to believe in. All I had to do was bring any problem I had to the AA meeting, and receive guidance. The danger of course is, how would I know which was good guidance and which was not? The good rabbi answered that I would know good guidance when it hit me in my heart.

And it turned out that he was right. I got to test my new "Good Orderly Direction" God-idea, the following week.

Back when my parents disowned me, I was cut off from their medical insurance. While I was living in the halfway house, I received a hospital bill in the amount of about $5,000. In 1989, this was a lot of money. I was bereft. I sat in my room in the halfway house, still on welfare, wondering how I was going to pay off this bill. I did the only thing I knew to do. I took the bill and went to an AA meeting to get that "group of drunks" to give me some "Good Orderly Direction." And they over delivered!

They told me to write the hospital an honest letter. I had to explain that I was trying to put my life in order, and that I was happy to pay off the bill once I was back on my feet. They told me to send the letter and see what happened. A few weeks later, I received a response. The nuns at the Catholic hospital told me that my bill would be deemed paid-in-full if I continued to stay sober.

Now, I'm not saying that I began to believe in God because I got a bill waived. I began to believe in God because I followed the directions that were given to me. And the direction those people gave me, was spot on. Their direction instructed me to take actions that ran counter to what I thought they should be.

For instance, they taught me to come to an AA meeting, show up early, say thank you to the coffee maker and speaker. I had to volunteer and keep my word by showing up week after week because people were counting on me. I had to eventually get a job and get off welfare. I followed the direction given to me because, over time, I learned that correct thinking follows the taking of correct actions. I couldn't think my way into right acting, but I could act my way into correct thinking. And over time, my thinking began to straighten out.

I continued to receive guidance from my friend and rabbi. He never imposed any conditions of what I should believe in where God was concerned. Instead, he encouraged me to take the steps of AA and have my own experience with this God that I was slowly beginning to believe in and see the results of God working in my life.

Years later, AA led me back to Judaism. My family had welcomed me back into their lives and I began to pursue Jewish studies more seriously. I began to study Judaism with this new perspective. I was amazed to see how much of AA's spiritual principles were contained in the text of Talmud, Torah, and other writings. Although I had studied these as an adolescent, I missed most of the message of how beneficent and abundant God is. That God is indeed compassionate and kind. That God can accomplish for us, the seemingly impossible. That my job was to align with God's will for me and seek that truth in any way I could: through study, through teaching, and through having my own experience with God. Over time, I began to comprehend the language of our forefathers and foremothers as they strove to live with integrity and humility. Through practice, I began to trust that God was here and all I had to do was seek a connection to God.

Just as my rabbi-friend predicted, I would know guidance when I felt it. I started living with the purpose of being more of service to God and my fellows. The day came when I was cleaning my bathtub, on my knees, scrubbing. When suddenly, I felt this bolt of energy hit me in my heart. And I knew I had to pursue the rabbinate. Although it took a lot of work, energy, and patience, I got ordained from Hebrew Union College when I was fifteen years sober, and have worked in congregational life ever since.

Today, God is as much a part of my life as is food and sunshine. My soul suffers when I do not spend time with God each day. I don't have to commune with God in a yoga pose. Instead, I just spend quiet time alone each morning and evening and have a set time for prayer and meditation.

I had hoped to one day return to my rabbi-friend, to let him know of his influence on my life, but I had missed the chance. When I made inquiries to find him and reconnect, I learned that he had passed away a few years prior.

I know he would have been so proud to know of the influence he had on me, and planted the seeds of a life well-lived, in my early days of sobriety. He'd be happy to hear that I have made a life of service to others and have a true purpose. Today, I dispense "Good Orderly Direction" to others in AA whom I sponsor and offer spiritual guidance to my congregation.

In my heart, I choose to believe, he already knew.

In keeping with the 11th Tradition of anonymity in Alcoholics Anonymous, Andrea C. does not identify herself further here.

The Evolving Descriptions and Grammar of God

—Rabbi Micah Ellenson

God is the ineffable, creative, driving force of the universe in which we exist. Ultimately, God is beyond description. While many moderns, with our scientific world view, question the supernatural God who performs miracles, the struggle of how to comprehend the divine is not a new one. Throughout Jewish history, there have been innumerable ways of understanding God. Many of them work for moderns in part, but not as a whole.

Take, for example, the issue of God's greatness as presented in our daily liturgy. The Talmud cites Neh 8:6, "And Ezra blessed YHVH, the great ruler." Rav Giddel says this greatness refers to the power of God's Name. Rav Mattana claims that God's greatness is that God is Mighty and Awesome. The members of the Great Assembly claim that God's greatness is found in God's ability to conquer God's inclination and exercise patience towards the wicked.[1]

So, who is right? They all are, and they all are not. Whatever attributes one ascribes to God cannot be enough. The Rabbis understand that due to the limited nature of our own perception we can never adequately describe God.

We attempt to understand God so that we can better apprehend the unknown and the nature of our relationship with the universe. The attempt also impresses upon us that we are part of something greater than ourselves. Modern knowledge helps us conceptualize God more scientifically than our ancestors. A modern understanding of God built on the shoulders

---

1. b. Yoma 69b.

of our ancestors can allow us to see that the universe is not random chaos, but an ordered design.

For example, scientists once thought that electrons were particles and crafted models of the electron based on that premise. They subsequently discovered that electrons could also act like waves. They later discovered that electrons sometimes acted like both. What scientists thought was true and the language they used to describe electrons had to evolve and be altered.

This is comparable to how humanity has approached God. For centuries we have used a particular grammar and understanding to describe God's nature. There is a passage by author Amos Oz that I read at every Friday night service:

> "I know that the tide is not an independent force, but merely the submission of the water to the movement of the moon in its orbit. And this orbit in its turn is subject to other orbits which are mightier far than it. And so the whole universe is held fast in the clinging grip of strong hands, the forces of Earth and Sun, planets, and comets, and galaxies, blindly erupting forces ceaselessly stirring in ripples of silence to the very depth of black space."[2]

These verses serve as a gateway to an understanding of God as the conscious force of the universe. In this understanding, the universe is viewed as a living organism of which we are a part. This "consciousness of the universe" becomes a synonym for God. The force which tells the tree to grow, to evolve and adapt, that spark, or biological drive and awareness, is not happenstance, it is God. God is the central nervous system and soul of the universe. In this schema, God can be understood as the creative awareness and driving force that causes the laws of physics, chemistry, and biology to move from idea (like potential energy) to actuality (like kinetic energy).

As beings consisting primarily of matter, we perceive four dimensions: height, length, width, and time. Geometrically speaking, we can conceive of these dimensions as the parts of a cube.

But imagine now that we exist in more than four dimensions, but our limited perception allows us to only experience four. Now imagine that you have traveled from our planet to a place beyond our universe, and are looking at all of creation from the outside. We are now looking at a shape. We have no idea what we are looking at, but it is something. The nature of

2. Frishman, *Mishkan T'filah*, 149.

this object is known on some levels (height, length, width, and time) and unknown on others.

God is much like this shape we are looking at, of which we can only perceive four of the dimensions. This can serve as our metaphor for God: God as a pan-dimensional being, unlike anything we can perceive due to our limited capacities. God as the consciousness of this shape, not a being outside this shape, animating that which goes on inside.

Throughout history, humanity has imagined God's desires by conceiving of God with a human personality and projecting our own aspirations onto God's mind. Hence the commandments calling us to live lives of justice, righteousness, charity, etc. Even when later understandings acknowledged God to be an incorporeal being, references to God with a personal pronoun, and as a proper noun, remained.

Consider Gen 1:26: "And God said, 'Let us make humans in our image, after our likeness.'" This verse reflects our earliest attempt at understanding how the universe worked and how God worked in it. In this conception, God was like us but not us. God was alien in nature but human in form.

Moreover, God was sometimes understood as a humanoid being with a name. Consider Exod 15:3, in which God is described as a warrior, "YHVH is a man of war, YHVH is his [God's] name." Like Zeus, Ra, or Odin, the ancient Israelites perceived their God in the same way. YHVH is the proper name of God. Not only did the Israelite God have a name, but he (and it probably was a he from the perspective of the Biblical authors) also had a home. That home was in the mountains, among the heavens, as we see in Ps 121:1–2:

> "I will lift up mine eyes unto the mountains: from whence shall my help come? My help comes from the LORD, who made heaven and earth."

All this is to say that the ancient way of interpreting and understanding the universe was that it was run by giant human-like beings who would come down from the heavens and either help or interfere in human life, for better or worse.

In a world of limited knowledge and understanding, with specific needs, this conception of God worked and worked well. However, as humanity expanded and discovered more about the nature of the world, science, and the universe, imagining God as a super-man living atop a mountain was no longer sufficient or believable.

Moses Maimonides, the great twelfth-century philosopher, doctor, and rabbi attempted to reconcile how the God concepts of Jewish tradition aligned with the evolving scientific and philosophical understandings of his day. He accomplished this by teaching that we need to understand the anthropomorphic descriptions of God in the Bible as metaphors for a being that was far greater than humans can imagine.

Maimonides attempts to explain the way we should understand God in many works. However, two of his ideas, in particular, can help shape our modern understanding of God:

> "God is one... His unity is unlike the unity of anything else that exists in the world. . . Rather, His unity is such that there is no unity like His in the world. If so [that God does not have a body], what does it mean that in the Torah, "And beneath His feet" (Exod 24:10)? . . . This accords to the thought of man, who can only comprehend bodies. And the Torah spoke in the language of man. And these are all epithets . . . a parable, and these are all parables. . . And the truth of the matter is that the mind of man is incapable of investigating Him or studying Him. And this is what the Scripture said (Job 11:7), "Can you by searching find out God? Can you find out the limit of the Almighty?"[3]

As humans, we can only apprehend God through metaphor because God is not a thing in the traditional sense. Unlike a chair, car, or tree we cannot experience God with our senses. God is unlike anything else in the universe.

The mystical idea of God as אין--*Ayin*–nothingness attempts to capture God's unique state as a noun describing a thing. In the mystical imagination, there are two aspects of existence, יש--*Yesh* and *Ayin*. *Yesh* refers to that which is and refers to all in the universe that possess thing-ness, i.e., matter. On the other side of *Yesh*, there is the world of *Ayin*, nothing. Although, it is better not to think of *Ayin* as "nothing," but as "no-thing." God is not "nothing," God is *Ayin*, no-thing. God then, too, is a thing, but a thing unlike any other thing. God is a no-thing. God's nature is no-thing-ness.

With this working description of what God is, let us explore how God works. Rabbi Harold Schulweis suggests that to understand God's nature we need to shift our outlook from God as a noun to God as a verb. He refers to this understanding of God's nature as *Elohut*, a verb meaning Godliness. This is in distinction to *Elohim*, a noun for God meaning Ruler.

---

3. *Mishneh Torah*: Foundations of the Torah, I:7, 9.

"To believe in Godliness is to believe in the verbs and adverbs that refer to the activities of divinity. To behave in a Godly fashion is to realize in one's life the attributes of Godliness that are potential in all human and non-human energies . . . the questions to be asked of those who seek God is not whether they believe in a noun that cannot be known but whether they can believe in the gerunds of Godliness: healing the sick, feeding the hungry, clothing the naked…"[4]

Per Schulweis, God is not a thing, a person, or a place, but the application of a just action. In many ways, Godliness makes the actions of life the reward of life. When we act justly, we are God-ing, if you will, and it is through imitation of God that we come to know how God operates in the universe.

At the same time, we are acting like God when we create, which some might say is God's defining attribute. As Joseph Soloveitchik describes in his essay *The Lonely Man of Faith,* the first human in the first chapter of Genesis attempts to know God by attempting to create like God.

"His motto is success, triumph over the cosmic forces. He engages in creative work, trying to imitate his Maker (*imitatio Dei*)."[5]

When we create, build, master, or act as a creative force, we are imitating the cosmic actions of God. In so doing, we connect with God. By understanding an aspect of God as a verb, we come to know God by doing as God does.

———————

We have no choice but to use human words to describe God. However, we must also recognize that these words only approximate descriptions of the eternal. Language by its nature is finite. God, by contrast, is infinite. Using finite words to describe an infinite being or force is, by its nature, paradoxical.

If we can begin to understand God dynamically and multidimensionally instead of statically, we will be better able to make a place for God in our world. God does not interact with the universe in just one way, but in many ways and all at once. It would behoove us to begin to conceptualize

4. Schulweis, *For Those Who Can't Believe,* 135.
5. Soloveitchik, *Lonely Man,* 17.

God in more complex, less limiting ways. We need to understand God, not as a mere metaphor, or verb, or pronoun. Rather we need to understand that God exists in all of these ways, and as a whole being that we cannot perceive with our senses alone.

Approaching God in this way, we can simultaneously engage in the dynamic nature of our own existence. We can begin to see that the tree provides shade and oxygen and grows according to a plan and design. The tree interacts with us but is not there solely for us. It is on its own path while it interacts with us on ours. To reduce God to any one of the concepts discussed above is to diminish our own existence in the vast, amazing, and complex universe in which we are blessed to live. This evolutionary understanding is not merely interesting, it is essential for our spiritual growth and development.

For many, the universe is a question of, "Is there a God or is there Science?" There needs to be enough room for an answer that allows for both God and Science. We can only come to a truer understanding of God if we are willing to shift our paradigms.

––––––––

Rabbi Micah Ellenson is the Rabbi of Temple Beth David in Cheshire, Connecticut, where he lives with his wife Sara, and two daughters, Lily and Rose. He received *smicha* and a Master's in Hebrew Letters from Hebrew Union College-Jewish Institute of Religion in 2014. He also holds a Bachelor in Psychology degree from the University of Southern California, and a Masters in Education from the American Jewish University in Los Angeles.

Judaism, Science, and God

—Rabbi Geoffrey A. Mitelman

In an ideal world, science would give us a full and accurate representation of the world, and people would simply accept those findings. Facts would be indisputable, and we would have a shared vision of truth. Yet as COVID, climate change, and teaching evolution have shown us, that's not the world we live in. One reason is that science *can't* ever give us a complete understanding of the natural world since science isn't a set of static facts; it's a process by which we better understand phenomena. But the second reason is a more complicated one, because questions surrounding topics that are fully accepted in the scientific community, such as the efficacy of vaccines, the role of humanity in warming the planet, or the role of natural selection in biological evolution, remain hot button issues in American society.

In the United States, there is a perception that when it comes to these questions, there are two sides that are in constant opposition—one side is viewed as scientific, liberal, and educated; the other is seen as religious, conservative, and uneducated. Not only that, there's a belief that if you pick anything from either column, you've got to pick everything from that column, and it's even better if you demonize the other side. Our public discourse has gone from, "You might have a point," to "I'm right" to "I'm right and you're wrong" to "I'm right and you're stupid" to "I'm right and you're evil."

This leads to a major problem in the Jewish community, especially when it comes to questions of belief and identity. Almost all non-Orthodox Jews (and even a significant number of Orthodox Jews!) pride themselves on being liberal, educated, and, as became a common refrain in 2020, people who "follow the science." Nearly three-quarters of non-Orthodox Jews identify as either politically moderate or liberal, and nearly 60% have at least a college degree (as compared to 30% in the rest of America).[1] With this "scientific/educated/liberal" v. "religious/uneducated/conservative" paradigm that dominates our intellectual landscape, if science is opposed to religion, then many Jews would say, "I don't want my science and my Judaism mixed." And if religion is opposed to science, then "I don't want any part of Judaism." Perhaps that's why a common refrain in liberal Jewish circles is some form of the phrase, "I don't believe in God, I believe in science." If science is seen as opposed to religion, then almost by definition, Jews will feel, at best, conflicted, and at worst, actively hostile about their sense of Jewish identity, beliefs, and feelings about God.

This challenge is part of a larger sociological trend and one that was the subject of a major study in 2015. The American Association for the Advancement of Science (the AAAS), the world's largest scientific organization, and Rice University partnered in a two-pronged initiative entitled "The Perceptions Project." It entailed both a survey on religion and science, as well as conversations and meetings to help both scientists and religious leaders better understand one another. They surveyed 10,000 Americans—Jews, Evangelical Christians, Catholics, and more—to provide a snapshot of religious communities' views on science, and then ran multiple, local small group conversations for members of the various religious perspectives. For the Jewish community, there were some surprising findings.

The first was that many of us erroneously think that Jews don't feel the same conflict between religion and science that, say, the evangelical Christian community feels. But in fact, about 25% of Jews *do* see religion and science as being in opposition—about the same number as the American population as a whole, and the same number as the evangelicals. Yet while most of the Christians who see religion and science as being in opposition view themselves as on the side of religion, those Jews who see science and religion in conflict come down on the side of science—and by a huge margin. For those "conflicted Christians," about three out of four opt for religion. But for those conflicted Jews, *fifteen out of sixteen* would see themselves on the side of science, and therefore, anti-religion. In other words, the problem isn't how to get Jews excited about science, it's how to get them excited about Judaism.

---

1. Pew Research Center, *Jewish Americans in 2020*, Ch. 2.

But there was a second, more subtle, conclusion for the Jewish community. Besides conflict, the Perceptions Project also offered respondents two other frameworks to describe the relationship between science and religion. People also had the option to say that these two realms were independent (referring to different aspects of reality) or collaborative (they can help support each other). Among all religious groups, Jews were both most likely to pick independent and least likely to pick collaborative to describe the relationship between religion and science. That is, *every other religious group* was more likely to hold that science could enhance their religious outlook than the Jewish community. Instead, Jews were much more likely to separate their religious and scientific outlooks and keep them siloed.[2]

While there are a myriad of historical and sociological reasons that Jews have a unique view of science, there are also theological reasons, which are worth exploring here. When most Americans talk about religion, the default assumption is Christianity, and in particular, white Protestant Christianity. Judaism, however, approaches questions of theology from a different perspective. Rather than a focus on faith (as Protestant Christianity often does), Jewish theology manifests itself in action, which requires debate, discussion, and logic. For example, there's a phrase that recurs all the time in Rabbinic literature: "*Min ayin*—How do we know this?" The Rabbis always had to explain their reasoning. And if there was a choice between believing something because of a Divine miracle or believing something because of thoughtful and reasoned arguments, there was no question which one the Rabbis would accept. Reason and logic would always win.

The classic story about this comes from the Talmud in the tale of the oven of Akhnai. As the story goes, Rabbi Eliezer was arguing with all the other Rabbis about a minute detail of Jewish law (trying to determine if a particular type of oven was kosher or not), and tried to convince them all that he was right, but his methodology was seen as faulty:

> ". . . Rabbi Eliezer brought forward every imaginable argument, but the Rabbis did not accept any of them. Finally, he said to them, "If I am right, let this carob tree prove it!" Sure enough, the carob tree immediately uprooted itself and moved one hundred cubits, and some say 400 cubits, from its place. "No proof can be brought from a carob tree," the Rabbis retorted.

2. AAAS, "Perceptions," 8–9.

And again he said to them "If I am right, let this river prove it!" Sure enough, the river of water flowed backward. "No proof can be brought from a river," they rejoined. . .

Finally, Rabbi Eliezer then said, "If I am right, let God prove it!" Sure enough, a Divine voice cried out, "Why are you arguing with Rabbi Eliezer? He is always right!" Rabbi Joshua then stood up and protested, "The Torah is not in heaven! We pay no attention to a Divine voice, [because now that the Torah has been given to humanity, people are the ones who are to interpret it.]"[3]

So even though the Torah was seen to be a gift from God and sacred scripture, as soon as the Torah had been given to humans, any arguments would have to be settled by logic and reason and would trump even a voice from God. Miracles might be wondrous, but they could never act as proof. When it comes to determining the nature of reality, we don't look to the supernatural.

Similarly, science never takes anything "on faith." Science is about continually questioning assumptions, revising theories, and integrating new data. Critical thinking is an essential aspect of science and is likewise deeply rooted in Jewish tradition. Indeed, perhaps the most important question science poses is, "How do we know this?"

This leads to a particularly Jewish way to think about God, especially in relation to science. As the Yiddish expression says, "If I knew God, I'd be God," so claiming that you know God's will is an act of incredible hubris. Instead, what we say about God has much more to say about us than it says about God. One way to approach questions of God, then, is through process theology, and one that is particularly consonant with scientific thinking.[4]

Science, at its best, is more of a dynamic way of understanding the world than compiling an eternal set of facts. It's a methodology and a way of approaching the world with a level of intellectual humility. And while both religion and science can fall into the trap of claiming certainty (such as the bumper sticker slogan "God says it, I believe it, That settles it"), at their best, they approach knowledge with an understanding that it will change over time.

A great example of how scientific knowledge progressed over the centuries is to ask the question, "What do we know about the earth?" If you had

---

3. b. B. Metz. 59b.

4. For those who want to learn more about Judaism and process theology, consider the writings of Rabbi Bradley Shavit Artson, more especially his book *Renewing the Process of Creation: A Jewish Integration of Science and Spirit*.

asked that question to people in the 1400s, they would have told you that they "knew" that the earth was the center of the universe. If you had asked Lord Kelvin, one of the greatest scientific minds of the nineteenth century, he would have told you that he "knew" that the earth was between 20 and 400 million years old. And if you had asked that question to most geologists in the early 20th century, they would have told you that they "knew" that the earth's continents were fixed in place. And of course, we now realize that what all these people "knew" about the earth was completely wrong.

On one level, the earth has been whatever the earth has been over its billions of years of history. But what has changed over just centuries is our *understanding* of what the earth is. In other words, the earth as an *actual object, in reality,* is different from the earth as we know it *at any given moment*. Indeed, everything scientific, such as the earth, the sun, atoms, genes, the universe, or humanity, lives in these same two worlds: what it is in reality and what we understand about it right now.

Professor Steven Goldman highlights this dichotomy in his outstanding course for the Teaching Company entitled "Science Wars: What Scientists Know and How They Know It." On the one hand, science is an attempt to give us clearer, better, and more accurate descriptions of the universe—a striving for a Platonic ideal. On the other hand, science is historical and temporal. New data, new instruments, new analyses, and new interpretations can and will change how we understand everything around us.

To help resolve that conflict, Goldman suggests that we view things like the earth, the sun, or atoms as "scientific objects." As he explains:

> It is much less controversial and difficult for us to grasp that "scientific objects" are redefined as we improve, as we get more experience, as we accumulate new data, we make new experiments. We have to redefine [these objects]—we sharpen the definition or throw it out and start with a new definition. That's different from changing Reality [sic], because our intuition is that what we mean by "Reality" is something changeless. . .
>
> [Seeing] scientific knowledge as about actualities ["scientific objects"] is a potentially useful way of eliminating much of the controversy from trying to understand the status of scientific knowledge and truth claims. At a minimum, scientific objects are justifiable instrumentally. What the implications of this instrumental success are vis-a-vis Reality is a separate issue.[5]

5. Goldman, "Science Wars", Lecture 24.

As Goldman argues, this idea of a "scientific object" is tremendously valuable. It helps us realize that we have to hold our beliefs about the world lightly, and at the same time, even as we know that these beliefs are imperfect, they form the lens through which way we look at and live in the world. Along those lines, I've grown to like the metaphor of God as a "scientific object."

Now, I am not suggesting God can be studied scientifically, or that if we find enough evidence we can prove (or disprove) God's existence, or that anything we don't understand yet is the result of God's handiwork. But those claims are not what this metaphor implies. Rather, I am saying that in the same way that we shouldn't focus on the earth in Reality (because we will never understand the earth in that way) and instead focus on the earth as we understand it right now, which can change based on new knowledge, similarly, we shouldn't focus on God in Reality (because we will never understand God in that way), and instead focus on God as we understand the Divine right now, which can change and grow based on new knowledge.

We hold certain beliefs, including beliefs about God—in particular, who or what God is (or is not) and how God acts (or doesn't act) in the world. But what doesn't happen often enough, whether someone is a fundamentalist, an atheist, or anything in between, is a willingness to rethink what we believe about God based on new ideas and new experiences. What we need is a working definition of "God," a theology that can change and adapt based on new data and new experiences. Rather than saying either, "This is what God is, and I know that I am right," or "There is no God because I don't believe that there is an Omnipotent, Omnipresent, Omnibenevolent Being that created the universe and directly impacts the world today," we can instead say, "Given what I know and I believe at this moment, this is what I believe God is and how God acts in this world. But when new data or new experiences arise, I might need to change my outlook."

In other words, we can think of and talk about "God" in the same way scientists have thought of and talked about scientific objects throughout human history. After all, just as we have been willing and able to change what we "know" about the earth, about atoms, and about the universe, we have to be willing and able to change what we "know" about God, as well.

Indeed, this view of God is consistent with how Judaism views God in the Torah. The most common name that God gives Godself in the Torah is *YHVH*, and the four letters that make up the word *YHVH* (*yod, hay, vav, hay*) at times also acted as vowels. As Rabbi Lawrence Kushner once said, if you tried to pronounce a name that was all vowels, you'd risk serious respiratory injury.[6] But perhaps even more importantly, the name *YHVH* is actually a conflation of all the tenses of the Hebrew verb "to be." God's name could be seen as "was-is-will be," so God isn't something you can capture or name, God is only something you can experience. Rather than asking the question "Who (or What) is God?," a better question would be "*When* is God?"

And indeed, when Moses is at the burning bush, having just been told by God that he will be leading the Israelites out of Egypt, he says, "Suppose I go to the Israelites and say to them, 'The God of your fathers has sent me to you,' and they ask me, 'What is his name?' Then what shall I tell them?" God responds that God's name is "*Ehyeh asher Ehyeh*," which is often translated as "I am what I am," but could also be translated as "I am what I will be." (Exodus 3:14) So God is whatever God will be—we simply have no idea. Indeed, for my own theology, I believe that God is found in the becoming, transforming "what will be" into "what is." Rather than seeing God as eternal and removed from the world, I experience God in the process, doing the work of bringing more justice and peace into this world.

Science, too, is very much about process. Science at its best is about testing hypotheses, setting up experiments, and exploring ideas. And if new data or new evidence arises, scientific knowledge changes. Science can't be tied down to old theories; it is dynamic and ever-changing. Just like our experience of God.

And perhaps that's how science and religion can be reconciled, not as two realms that are in conflict or as "non-overlapping magisteria" (as Stephen Jay Gould once described them), but as things you do. The perceived conflict between religion and science is more of a historical and sociological phenomenon, rather than a theological or philosophical one. If we can approach both questions of science and Judaism with a level of humility, openness, and willingness to change, we can move beyond simplistic "either/or" dichotomies, and discover new ways to approach other people, Jewish tradition, and God.[7]

---

6. Kushner, *Eyes Remade*, 144.

7. Elements of this chapter have been adapted from the author's selected previous writings on sinaiandsynapses.org, as well as from the chapter "Science and Truth" in *These Truths We Hold*, forthcoming by HUC Press.

Rabbi Geoffrey A. Mitelman is the Founding Director of Sinai and Synapses, an organization that bridges the scientific and religious worlds, and is being incubated at Clal—The National Jewish Center for Learning and Leadership. His work has been supported by the John Templeton Foundation and is an internationally sought-out teacher, presenter, and scholar-in-residence.

A Philosopher Explains What Belief in God Means

—Rabbi Elliot N. Dorff

WE HUMAN BEINGS EXPERIENCE the world on three different levels. The first is the concrete level that we experience through our five senses. This includes such diverse things as tables, songs, and people.

Even on this level, it is harder than you might first think precisely to define what is, for example, a table. Is it a flat surface with legs? But so is a chair! And what about the tables in restaurant booths that are screwed into the wall and have no legs? If instead of defining a table in terms of its form you want to define it in terms of its function – e.g., a table is a surface on which to put things – how is that different from a desk? Or even a floor? At this point we are talking only about a table, where we are pretty confident that we know what we are talking about. What if instead we were talking about a song? How would you differentiate a song from noise, especially given people's diverse tastes in music and the existence of atonal music? So even on the concrete level, being able to describe precisely what you mean can be difficult. When asked to define many elements of the concrete world and finding it impossible to be precise, one is sorely tempted give up and fall back on Justice Potter Stewart's comment about obscenity (in the United States Supreme Court's case, *Jacobellis v. Ohio* (378 U.S. 197 [1964]) when he could not define that precisely, "I know it when I see it."

Defining precisely what you mean becomes even harder on the second level of experience that we humans have, the first level of abstraction. This level includes some very important aspects of our life that have major impacts on its shape and quality but which we do not experience directly with our five senses, although we do see concrete examples of all of these abstract entities. Examples of this level include justice, goodness, truth, beauty, and all of our associations (e.g., family, friendship, nationhood, etc.) Defining justice is the subject of one of the very first books of Western philosophy, Plato's *Republic*, and philosophers, jurists, and legislators have struggled to define it in both theory and practice ever since. There are similarly varying theories of truth (e.g., the correspondence theory vs. the coherence theory), and even a broader set of theories about what constitutes beauty. Modern DNA testing has revealed that some of us are related to people we never would have guessed are members of our family. Adopted children and children created through donor sperm or eggs need to differentiate those who are their family genetically in contrast to those who are their family socially, including the ones who put in the time, effort, and resources to raise them. So defining "family" is also more complicated than one might imagine.

It should not be surprising, then, that precise definitions are even more difficult when it comes to the third level of human experience, the second level of abstraction. This is sometimes described as "the transcendent," or "ultimate reality." It is often conceived as the container of all of our experiences. Philosophers try to describe it in the area of philosophy known as metaphysics, which Aristotle, in his book, *Metaphysics*, called "the queen of the sciences." As is typical for philosophy, the goal of those thinking and writing in metaphysics is descriptive and analytic: what is the phenomenon that we experience, how does it function, and how is it different from, and related to, other phenomena that we experience?

Like philosophy, the religions of the world think deeply about all three levels of human experience, but they do so with a different goal that is captured in the very word "religion." The "lig" in that word comes from the Latin word, *ligare*, which means to connect, tie, or bond. That Latin root also appears in the English word "ligament," which can be any connection but in medicine is specifically the connective tissue that binds one bone to another; similarly, when a woman has had as many children as she wants, she sometimes has her tubes tied, called medically "a tubal ligation," Religions, then, etymologically and in practice, are interested not so much in *describing* and *analyzing* the three levels of our experience, which are the central goals of philosophy, but rather in fostering our *connections* to all three levels.

So, in the concrete world, religions concern themselves with creating and shaping our interactions with the environment and the people within it. Some of the ways that religions do this are: (1) rituals to call our attention to, and mark the change of, the seasons and the life cycle and/or to bring us together as families and communities; (2) art, music, literature, and dance to help us make an art of life; (3) stories to articulate our sense of historical connection to our past, present, and future; and (4) moral norms that are taught in educational materials, sermons, and environments (schools, camps, youth groups, houses of worship) to guide our interactions with each other in every aspect of life and to motivate us do what we can to eliminate or at least ameliorate the moral problems of everyday life, including poverty, illness, prejudice, etc.

On the first level of abstraction, religions provide both materials and formats to bring us together to discuss what a given religious group's stance should be on moral issues. Among the issues discussed most in religious settings these days are climate change; poverty; prejudice; inequity in housing, education, health care, and jobs; immigration; sexual ethics; business ethics; the proper and improper use of social media; and medical issues at the beginning and end of life. Grappling with such issues in light of each religion's vision of what is a good human being and a good society, as well as its more concrete articulations of what that vision entails in practice, is a major function of religion.

Another issue on this first level of abstraction is the relationships that a particular religious group should have with other religious and secular groups. Putting it starkly, if we believe that x is true and good, do we have enough humility to believe that other groups who see things differently can nevertheless consist of smart and moral people and deserve to be respected as such—hopefully to the point of entering into respectful dialogue and maybe then mutual action but at least friendly disagreement?

It is on the second level of abstraction that the word "God" appears in religious language. That word is defined in many ways, but two common ones are these: a separate being with a will and personality who created and sustains the universe and who actively interacts with it and cares about it ("theism"); or, alternatively, the force that created the world and sustains it, or that is the world ("deism"). Each of these two major groups has subsets. So, for example, there are rationalists and existentialists among theists, and among deists there are those who think that the world has been created in a particular time and is static (e.g., Platonists) and those who think that the process of creation is dynamic and ongoing (Aristotelians, including, but not limited to, "Process theology.") Religions use the word "God" or some other name or metaphor, rather than just saying, "the transcendent" or "ultimate reality," because, again, they aim to help us *relate* to that reality, not just describe or analyze it, and it is much easier to relate to the world if it is imagined in an anthropomorphic image or some other concrete term.

Precisely because we are talking about the second level of abstraction, precise descriptions of that ultimate reality, let alone precise definitions of it, are not just difficult, but impossible. That is expressed in theological language as God being "holy," that is, wholly other than anything we human beings can comprehend. It is important to state clearly that recognizing God as holy should not stop us from learning whatever we can about the world on all three levels of experience that we have of it. On the contrary, if God created the world, then learning more about it through the various relevant sciences is also learning more about God's plan for us who live in it. So the recognition of God's holiness should not deter us from studying all aspects of the world that affect us or from trying to live in it more robustly through whatever changes we make, taking into account, as we must, the need to preserve the world as well as to manipulate it for our purposes. While doing that, though, the recognition of God's holiness should make us aware of the awesome nature of the universe, our dependence on it, and our inability to comprehend it all, thus fostering in us a sense of humility and gratitude.

God's holiness should also inspire us to live a righteous life. Leviticus 19 makes this clear: one of the opening verses, with "you" and "shall be" in the plural and so addressed to the entire People Israel, asserts: "You shall be holy, as I, the Lord, your God, am holy" (19:2). That verse serves as a header for the rest of the chapter that defines at least part of what holiness entails, including respect for parents, taking care of the poor, having honest weights and measures, coming to the rescue of those in distress, observing one day a week as the Sabbath so that work does not become an idol, refraining from vengeance and bearing a grudge and instead reproving someone who needs rebuke, and, ultimately, "Love your neighbor as yourself." (Lev 19:18) As a society, we should strive to become "a kingdom of priests and a holy nation." (Exodus 19:6) So the point of relating to God is not just to gain knowledge; it is to model ourselves after God and thus become better individuals and communities.

We find it easier to relate to God—that is, the transcendent element of our experience, ultimate reality—through metaphors that make it possible for us not only to understand what we can, but also to relate to it., and so the Bible itself refers to God in many ways. One is the generic word "god" (*el* or *elohim* in Hebrew) and God's proper name (the tetragrammaton of four Hebrew letters, *yod, heh, vav, heh*, but pronounced as *Adonai,* my Lord, as a matter of respect, much as we call our parents "Mother" and "Father" or the affectionate "Mom" or "Dad" rather than by their proper names). In addition to these generic and proper names for God, the Bible refers to God through multiple metaphors, as, for example, Father and Creator (Deuteronomy 32:6), Sun and Shield (Ps 84:11); and eight metaphors in two consecutive verses (Ps 18:2–3): "I adore you, O Lord (the tetragrammaton), my strength, my crag, my fortress, my rescuer, my God, my rock in whom I seek refuge, my shield, my mighty champion, my haven. Then, of course, there is the famous verse, "The Lord is my shepherd. . ." (Ps 23:1) These are all partial windows into the nature of God. The classical Rabbis aptly name this higher level of abstraction "the Place" (*ha-Makom*), asserting that, "The Holy Blessed One is the place of His universe, but His universe is not His place;" (*Genesis Rabbah* 68:9) that God encompasses space, but space does not encompass God.

What does it mean, then, *not* to believe in God? It could mean that one is blind to the third level abstraction altogether, that one lives one's life on the concrete level alone or perhaps also on the first level of abstraction. Alternatively, it could mean that one experiences the second level of abstraction, but it does not matter much in a given person's life. Most often, I think, it means that someone identifies God with a particular metaphor or vision of God that has not panned out in his or her life, especially when they prayed to God for something that did not happen, and then they become an agnostic or atheist because that particular understanding of God did not materialize. In those cases, one may want to rethink the ways in which one understands God rather than ignore or deny one's experience of transcendence. In particular, as the classical Rabbis already assert, a prayer to reverse something that has already happened is a vain prayer (M. *Berakhot 9:3*), and they also assert that we may not depend on miracles in the sense of violations of the laws of nature (B. *Kiddushin* 39b), and therefore should not expect prayers that such miracles occur to be fulfilled. (That is very different from our daily prayer in the Amidah to thank God for "Your miracles that are daily with us," where the "miracles" are the laws of nature that enable us to live and function.)

Conversely, what does it mean to believe in God? It is to be aware of the second level of abstraction and to make it an important part of how one understands oneself and lives one's life. The metaphors by which one refers to that level of experience will undoubtedly change over time and as one gains experience with all levels of experience. Martin Buber made an important distinction between "belief *that*" something is the case, which he called p-faith for the Greek word *pistis,* knowledge, in contrast to "belief *in*" something or someone, which he called e-faith, from the Hebrew word *emunah,* meaning trust. His point is that belief in God is not so much a matter of assertions *that* the world and anything beyond it is of a particular nature, although belief in God does entail the assertion that we human beings do indeed have the third level of experience as well as the other two. Belief in God, though, is more a statement that one's experience of the transcendent, the second level of abstraction, can be trusted to be real and true, and that one should therefore live one's life with humility, gratitude, morality, and aspirations for holiness.

Rabbi Elliot N. Dorff, Ph.D., is the Rector and Distinguished Service Professor of Philosophy at American Jewish University and the author of *Knowing God: Jewish Journeys to the Unknowable.* His publications include over two hundred articles on Jewish thought, law, and ethics, together with fourteen books that he has written and an additional fourteen books that he has edited or co-edited on those topics.

PART II

BELIEVABLE WORDS

Prayerbook Problems—and Solutions

—Rabbi Richard Agler

The *Siddur* is the traditional gateway to Jewish life, belief, and practice. The prayers it contains, the statements it makes, and the faith it describes are understood, as much as any one volume can be, as Judaism's "official word." Yet much remains in *siddurim* and *mahzorim* (High Holyday prayerbooks) that attests to beliefs and understandings that large numbers of twenty-first-century Jews no longer accept. As a result, in many congregations, the sanctuary is the least crowded space in the synagogue.

The books are filled with prayers that ask God to overturn the laws of nature. There are assurances that God protects people who are good. There are prayers that ask God to "come down" and change the course of history. There is testimony that God determines, justly of course, our fate. Each of these perceptions has been challenged and repudiated by our accumulated life experience and our reason. The disconnect between the contents of the *siddur*[1] and what educated Jews in reality believe is significant.

As Jewish belief has evolved through history, prayers have evolved as well. In recent centuries, *siddurim* have been modified to reflect contemporary perspectives on animal sacrifice, bodily resurrection, the use of the vernacular, the nature of the messiah, Jewish chosen-ness, Zionism, the length of the service, gender, and more.

More recent revisions have included the addition of poetic, spiritual, and other inspirational readings and commentaries. But most of the ancient and medieval God-ideas remain in place. And the *siddur* communicates them clearly. It is time to give contemporary Jews a *siddur* with a living,

---

1. For the remainder of this essay, references to the *siddur* should be understood to include the *mahzor* as well.

non-mythical God at its heart. What follows outlines where we fall short and how we might do better.

Tefilot Shav—תפילות שוא—Empty Prayers

The *Mishnah* teaches that prayers asking God to change outcomes that have already been determined are *tefilot shav*—empty, vain, or futile prayers.[2] Someone returning to his town who sees a house burning in the distance and prays that the fire not be in his home is making a *tefilat shav*—an empty prayer. The fire's location has already been determined and, the Rabbis understood, it was beyond the power of prayer to change it. Similarly, if expectant parents pray that the sex of their *in utero* child be one or the other, that has likewise already been determined and cannot be changed by prayer. It, too, is a *tefilat shav*. Despite this classically Jewish and logical understanding, contemporary *siddurim* contain numerous prayers that might well be considered empty, vain, or futile.

Consider the pleas asking God to cure illness. They date to biblical accounts portraying God as the source of disease and recovery.[3] The Bible and Talmud suggest that when people pray on behalf of the sick, God can be moved to heal them.[4]

Moderns understand that this is not how disease works. The condition of the patient, the skill of the physicians, the medicines administered, and (God's) laws of biology, chemistry, and nature are what determine an illness' outcome. Prayer plays a supporting role, at best. If the classical Rabbis understood science as we do, they too would have considered petitions asking God to "come down and heal" to be prayers in vain.

The *siddur*, of all books, should not portray prayer as capable of doing what it cannot. When people see that prescribed prayers fail to alter the course of nature, it undermines, instead of strengthens, their relationship with God. There are prayers that we can, and should, offer on behalf of the sick but, "God, please heal her," is not one of them.

It is true that moral support can be a critical factor in the treatment of serious, and even not-so-serious, illness. When patients are aware that others are concerned enough to pray for them, they are often comforted. This can aid in the healing process. While the prayer itself may have no effect

2. m. Ber. 9:3.

3. Job 5:18; b. Ket. 104a.

4. e.g., Num 12:13.

either on the disease or on God, praying for the sick can give the pray-er comfort as well. Sometimes it is the only thing we can do for our dear ones. Our written prayers can be reframed to reflect this reality.

Siddurim are similarly filled with petitions asking God to grant us peace. But these, too, are prayers in vain. When humanity remains intent on disturbing the peace it is beyond the power of God to bestow it upon us.[5] Nor does God change the behavior of others in response to our requests, however sincere or impassioned they may be. Instead of words like these, *siddurim* should offer prayers that encourage and inspire us to utilize our own strength to seek peace and pursue it. Some do, but such prayers are found in the same services as those addressed to a God who has the power to grant peace—or not. Confused? Who wouldn't be?

*Bakashot—*בקשות*—*Requests

Other prayers of doubtful efficacy are known in the tradition as *bakashot*. These are requests we make of God that can be found in every service, even on *Shabbat* and holidays when they are theoretically omitted.[6] *Bakashot* ask God to grant us things such as protection from harm, justice for the oppressed (and the oppressors), mercy for the deserving, victory over our enemies, bountiful harvests, improved self-control, numerous descendants, righteous leaders, and greater prosperity.

Bakashot prompt us to ask God for what we want with the expectation that God will tell us either yes or no. (Hopefully, yes.) They are also predi-cated on the belief that our prayers have agency, i.e., the power to change God's mind or course of action. And they also imply that God can alter the laws of nature on our behalf.[7]

Few, today, who are beyond the age of childhood believe that God acts in this way. *Bakashot*, like *tefilot shav*, may give voice to worthwhile desires but it is our responsibility, not God's, to fulfill them—if they can be fulfilled at all.

Asking God to do things for us, whether they fall within the possibil-ity of what physics and nature allow or not, carries within it significant potential for spiritual harm. When it appears that God has denied one of

---

5. b. Ber. 33b.

6. e.g., *R'tzeh*—רצה, *Sim Shalom*--שים שלום, *Hashkiveinu*--השכיבנו, many others.

7. e.g., כי אל פועל ישועות אתה—*Ki El Poel Yeshuot Atah*—You, O God, work to deliver us.

our requests, we may walk away feeling disappointed, rejected, alienated, or worse. It may leave us thinking that God did not find our prayers good enough, that God did not find us good enough, or perhaps that God does not even exist in the first place. Prayer should never point us in any of these directions.

Ancient legends notwithstanding, God has yet to answer a prayer to rescue a decent and righteous human life from danger through miraculous or supernatural intervention. The only possible explanations are that God has rejected us, God does not exist, or that this is not how God works. The latter is true. This is not how God works. God does not betray us[8]—although misdirected prayers may.

It is mistaken to ask, and wrong to expect, God to supernaturally intervene and magically do our work for us. Prayers that encourage such a mindset should be removed from our *siddurim*.

At the same time, *bakashot* can, and do, remind us of what is worthwhile and valuable. They articulate goals to which we can aspire and values we should strive to uphold. We would do better to think of them, and to phrase them, as requests we make of our higher selves—and of the Divine spirit within us.

Hashgaha—השגחה—Providence

Siddurim are also filled with affirmations of the ancient Jewish doctrine known as *hashgaha*. It is the belief that God watches over, cares for, and protects us—as individuals and as a people. At the same time, it holds that God has a plan through which He (*sic*) guides human history.[9] These are beliefs that many moderns reject. We understand why.

The idea of God as the protector and guardian of the innocent and righteous is impossible to square with all that we have seen and experienced. Far too many decent and upright individuals—of every faith and nation—have suffered cruelly, unjustly, and mercilessly. Entire peoples, including our own, have endured unspeakable catastrophe. Billions have now borne witness to this.

If the God of justice and love is overseeing and directing the course of history, then God is doing a poor job of it. Rather than accept this, we can

8. 1 Sam 15:29.
9. Malbim on Ps 33:14.

affirm that while the course of human destiny may depend on God's spirit, it rests very much on human will.

The Torah commands us to pursue justice and righteousness, to love our neighbors as we love ourselves, and to protect the powerless from the predations of the powerful. Clearly, the state and well-being of our world depends on us. Asking God to do our work misleads us, mischaracterizes God, and makes for deeply unsatisfying prayer.

THE SUPERNATURAL AND SUPERSTITIOUS

Texts conceived by the ancient religious imagination describing supernatural occurrences abound in classical Jewish literature. The preeminent twelfth-century philosopher and legal authority Moses Maimonides did not believe that they should be taken literally. Instead, he taught that "the Torah speaks in the language of humanity," i.e., metaphorically.[10] We appreciate that many of those ancient texts possess inspirational power, but most moderns are comfortable with Maimonides' understanding.

Yet, for example, *siddurim* traditionally contain prayers asking God to bring life-sustaining rain and dew to the Land of Israel. These are predicated on the ancestral belief that rain and dew are a reward for keeping the commandments.[11] Alas, we know differently. Rainfall and dew are determined by meteorological conditions and are not dependent, in any way, shape, or form, on how closely people adhere to the Torah's commandments. Moreover, the belief that God can be persuaded to make dew or rain fall when atmospheric conditions do not warrant them is, essentially, a superstitious one.

We do know, however, that human conduct has a profound effect on the overall health of the environment. The quality of our care for the earth, seas, and skies impact not only rain and dew, but the overall climate as well. Again, it is our responsibility, not God's, to be stewards of the planet.[12]

Siddurim also portray God as our *Shomer*—שומר, Guardian and Protector. This is an understanding that dates to the covenants described in the Torah between God and Abraham, and later, between God and the nation at Mt. Sinai. The fealty of our people to this covenant has been a hallmark of Jewish existence and survival. But this does not mean that God

10. *Mishneh Torah*, Foundational Laws of the Torah, 1:9.

11. Deut 11:13–14.

12. Gen 2:15; *Kohelet Rabbah* 7:13.

supernaturally protects us from harm as a reward for our dedication. History could not be more clear on this point. It is better to understand that commitment to God's path and way is its own reward,[13] without expectation for any *quid pro quo*.

WHAT *CAN* WE PRAY FOR?

If we eliminate prayers that are *tefilot shav, bakashot,* claim *hashgaha,* or rely upon superstitious or supernatural understandings of God, what might be left? A great deal, actually.

We can pray to be able to recognize God's presence in the works and laws of creation and in the spirit of holiness.

We can pray to make more of that spirit our own through acts of kindness, wisdom, truth, compassion, love, charity, and justice.

We can pray that we might draw more deeply upon our Jewish tradition as a source of moral and ethical counsel.

We can pray to be instilled with the spirit of gratitude for life and its blessings.

We can pray to strengthen our commitment to our achievable dreams and worthy hopes.

We can pray for the courage to persevere, to overcome fear, and to pass life's severest tests.

We can pray that we might find the path to our highest selves.

We can pray that we might be able to listen for the still, small voice that Elijah heard.[14]

We can pray to embrace more behaviors that point us towards holiness.

We can pray to understand how life can be an expression of divine service.

We can pray for the drive and wisdom to help us find a sacred community.

We can pray for a stronger desire to help heal and repair the world.

We can pray to better embrace the role and responsibility of the people of Israel to be a light unto the nations.

---

13. *Pirke Avot* 4:2.
14. 1 Kgs 19:12.

Richard Agler is the Founding Rabbi, now Rabbi Emeritus, of Congregation B'nai Israel in Boca Raton, FL, the Scholar Emeritus of the Keys Jewish Community Center/Congregation Ohr Hayam in Tavernier, FL, and the Co-Director of the Tali Fund, Inc. His book, *The Tragedy Test: Making Sense of Life-Changing Loss* (2018), delineates his understanding of God as Law and Spirit.

Prayer Can Transform—or Not

—Rabbi Samuel M. Cohon

"The one who rises from prayer a better person—that person's prayer has been answered."—Herman Wouk

Something is wrong with contemporary Jewish prayer.

When younger Jews participate actively in Jewish prayer experiences today, they do not, by and large, do so in established Reform, Conservative, Reconstructionist, Progressive or other non-Orthodox congregations. A look around any synagogue, or at Zoom screens or Facebook emojis, shows that the majority of people committed to regular Shabbat service attendance are older, often significantly so, than we would like to admit. Where are the younger people? Not, certainly, in our temples.

This trend has been accelerating for years. With the exception of the families of life-cycle celebrants or the relatives of performing students at made-to-order Religious School services, standard Jewish congregations on a typical Shabbat are made up of older Jews—and their parents. And grandparents. Shabbat service attendance, whether on Friday night for Reform Jews or Saturday morning for Conservative Jews, is simply no longer a regular practice.

The most "successful" synagogues located in major centers of the American Jewish world sometimes manage to attract a crowd, but that is usually by featuring a controversial speaker or putting on a special service with added musical or theatrical attractions. The tradition of coming to synagogue on *Shabbat* to pray, to talk to God using a set liturgical structure, has not been passed down to younger generations of Reform, Conservative, Reconstructionist and Progressive Jews.

Even the camp-style services that promised to transform the Jewish world a few decades ago are now largely populated by aging boomers in their seventies and eighties. The spiritual energy among younger Jews seeking religious community has migrated to independent *minyanim* [prayer groups] that avoid having professional clergy and to Orthodox services— but for most younger Jews it hasn't migrated at all. It's just not there.

Interestingly, that doesn't mean that most younger Jews lack spirituality, or they don't need to find a way to connect with God in a meaningful way. It's just that they likely seek it in ways other than prayer, or at least other than in Jewish prayer services in a Reform, Conservative, Progressive, Reconstructionist, Renewal, or unaffiliated non-Orthodox synagogue.

What, then, has replaced prayer as a form of spiritual expression? For some, it's the elevated personal experience of listening to music, particularly live music: rock concerts, country music, hip hop, jazz shows, or music festivals. For others, it's designating time for physical activity: running, biking, hiking, or swimming; replenishing spirit by generating endorphins. Still others find spiritual connection through the many available mindfulness apps, or by listening to spiritual podcasts or practicing areligious meditation.

The vast majority of contemporary Jews spend more time reading news feeds, checking social media, watching sports, or playing video games on cell phones than they ever do praying. They also spend more time exercising, figuring out what restaurant to go to, and kvetching about what's wrong with the world than trying to talk with God.

Which is what prayer is: focused conversation with God. That can take place at a synagogue Friday night or Saturday morning, at home when we arise or retire, when we travel, or at any time we choose. But the point is that we must, first, choose a time to do this, and actually make an effort to pray, to talk to God.

And younger contemporary non-Orthodox Jews are choosing simply not to do this at all. Why not?

Is it, perhaps, because of the words we are supposed to be saying when we pray?

"Liturgy recapitulates theology," a clever professor once said in my class at Hebrew Union College, paralleling Ernest Haeckel's dictum "ontogeny recapitulates phylogeny." That is, just as an organism theoretically reflects the entire evolutionary history of its species, prayer reflects the whole belief system of a religious group. If our *Siddur*, our prayer book, rooted in the themes of Creation, Revelation, and Redemption, and filled with blessings praising God for everything from opening our eyes to healing the sick to redeeming the captives to comforting the bereaved, were really to express what we believe today, would it read the way it does now?

Jewish prayer comes from a deep and nuanced tradition, and it is, as Christians say, liturgical in nature; there are words we are supposed to say, and the structure of most of those words has been established for thousands of years. Most non-Orthodox Jews—the vast majority of Jews around the world, including in Israel—know a few of these prayers well. Fewer know many prayers well, and a small percentage know nearly all of them well. When we pray, we are taught to use a set, ordered sequence of prayers to try to capture what our people believe as well as what rabbis and scholars decided was most important for us to say, and for God to hear from us. Those prayers, their order and frequency, were determined in part in *Masehet Berahot* in the Babylonian Talmud, codified around 450 CE. Subsequent *siddurim* further structured the service, and every prayer book since has followed along similar lines. Say this prayer first, that one next, conclude with these prayers and hymns.

The wise teachers who arranged the prayers in our *siddur*, and who also wrote some of the beautiful poetry that encompassed their own ideas about God, belief, and personal responsibility, created a treasure of literary and theological beauty. When you read or chant or sing the prayers of the *siddur*, either in the original Hebrew or Aramaic or in English translation or paraphrase, you are journeying through an entire empire of belief, meaning, theology, psychology, and history, joining our ancestors in a remarkable realm exploring the human experience of the divine. Some of the prayers in our *siddur* are masterpieces of religious creativity, while others find ways of speaking to our deepest needs, fears, and joys. The best do both with elegance and power.

But there is a serious problem today when we try to travel through this extraordinary masterpiece of prayer, this *siddur* of our people, for something other than historical tourism, something more than a Jewish Museum visit to the land of prayer. It is simply this: we don't speak the same language our ancestors did, and generally, we don't believe the same things they did about God, the universe, life after death, or even our own families and lives. And since prayer is supposed to express our beliefs, using a *siddur* predominantly derived from sources ranging from the sixth century BCE to the thirteenth century CE, with additions up to the nineteenth century, doesn't match our twenty-first-century needs. The beautiful language of these prayers, and it is often beautiful indeed, can't quite hide the fact that most of us just don't believe what many of the words say about the power of God in the world and in our lives.

When we begin the morning prayers, the *Birkot HaShahar*, thanking God for creating the rooster, which served as our ancestors' alarm clocks, we aren't reflecting a reality of our own digital world. When we effusively praise God and elucidate God's paramount perfection in prayers such as *Baruh She'amar*, or acknowledge God's omnipotent power in the *Yotzer* we speak only of a transcendent God who resides above us. Yet most contemporary Jews who believe in God conceive of God in a variety of ways that are barely articulated in the traditional *Siddur*, if they are present at all: the immanent God of *Kabbalah*, the existentialist God of twentieth-century Jewish theologians Franz Rosenzweig and Martin Buber, the immanent God of Abraham Joshua Heschel, the limited God of Harold Kushner. Where are the prayers that express these visions of the Divine?

This challenge is not merely the side-show problem that Hebrew is a gendered language and many Jewish prayers seem sexist in English translation. We've now witnessed generations of Reform and other non-Orthodox rabbis, cantors, and lay people obsessively focused on making language, prayer, and the professional experiences of Judaism more inclusive or gender-neutral or feminist. But in a larger sense, it is hard to understand why taking archaic ideas and language and dressing them up in non-gendered clothing will make the *siddur* any more referable and attractive to today's Jews.

We've also seen technology used to try to attract contemporary Jews: visual *tefilah*—slideshows or videos with prayer texts and various images projected overhead, Zoom and Facebook productions of carefully orchestrated musical and video performances that turn prayer into a spectator sport, and of course, the large folk-song-style singalong version of prayer. These are tools, perhaps helpful, but it remains to be seen how valuable they ultimately prove to be when they are, in essence, dressing up ideas and texts that simply may not speak to us today. You can take a prayer that says, "You God, show us great love by commanding us to observe your Torah and fulfill your commandments, ritual and pragmatic, that you teach us," add a sweet melody with pleasant guitars and modern harmonies, project it on a big screen with images of Israel or give it a Zoom background of happy little children, and you still have a text that doesn't express how most contemporary Jews—indeed, nearly all Conservative, Reform, Reconstructionist, Renewal and Progressive Jews—live their lives.

If prayer is a way to connect with what is most profoundly valuable and important in our lives, if it exists to reinforce our best impulses and help us overcome our worst ones, how can we recover a connection to the experience of prayer?

I have always been something of a traditionalist about Jewish prayer, exploring the ways its innate creative tension between individual and communal prayer, between a structured *siddur* and the need we have to talk openly and honestly with God in our own words, has served our people so well for so very long. But it is long past time to create a genuinely new approach to Jewish prayer for our generation and the generations that are coming, who don't have much, if any, connection to traditional words and, especially, to a theology they just don't share.

Does that mean that the eternal verities of prayer, the elegant balance between *keva*, fixed regular liturgical prayer, and *kavannah*, personal, spontaneous, emotional expression, has lost all value? Or is something to be done here besides throwing out the *berahot*—blessings, baby with the bathwater?

Having spent my entire life doing Jewish prayer, and forty-three years working as a cantor and rabbi, I've come to believe we need to explore something quite different going forward. We must choose to emphasize *Kavannah* in a far more central way. And however that transforms our experience of prayer, it must reflect what Jews really believe about God and our lives and our world today.

A personal anecdote: I grew up in a cantorial and rabbinic household, attended Jewish day school and Hebrew High, trained as a cantor myself, and have served congregations professionally from the time I was seventeen years old. After thirteen years as a cantor, seven full-time, I returned to HUC-JIR, served as a spiritual leader, student rabbi, and rabbinic intern, was ordained a rabbi at the age of thirty-four, and began serving as a congregational rabbi. Through all those years of education and experience, the very first time I was ever asked to offer a spontaneous prayer came at an interfaith gathering in my first official rabbinic pulpit.

Frankly, I had no idea what to do. I had always thought about prayer as something we did using the words of the *siddur*, or the *mahzor*, or perhaps a carefully worded text we created and honed before daring to use it in a public gathering. It never occurred to me that I should just dredge up whatever words came to mind and speak them to God in the moment.

In other words, based on my education and experience in the Jewish world, the very notion of *kavannah* [concentration] was divorced from what we might actually offer as prayer. You need special *kavannah* before you say the words of the *Sh'ma*, a series of quotations from the Torah in the liturgy. You need special *kavannah* when you *daven* the *Amidah,* the central prayer service. You should focus your attention on the holy words of the prayer book on the High Holy Days, of course. But *kavannah* never meant some sort of spontaneous outpouring to a listening Deity. It was not, "God, I am so sad today, and hope You will give me the strength to do the challenging tasks I have ahead of me." It was never, "God, I'm so grateful for my new job, and want things to go well." It wasn't even, "God, please give the surgeon the skill to perform the operation well."

But the truth is that the deepest and most personal prayers don't come out of prayer books. They come out of human hope and need, out of feelings of gratitude, sadness, desperation, exaltation. And if we are to connect younger people to prayer, they must also come out of words created and spoken today.

As someone who has edited and written prayer books, and led thousands of prayer services, I think something really needs to change in how we approach prayer in the future if we don't want our prayers to be limited to a kind of museum housing the dreams and beliefs of antique historic versions of Judaism that have no real, vital place in our lives now.

And that change must be a revival—in fact, a renaissance—of the ability to create new prayers, and an education that also gives Jews the skills to know how to pray spontaneously. It will require that we show people how prayer can, should, and must come from *kavannah*, their own feelings, needs, desires, and hopes.

It will only come when we empower our own Jews to seek and find words to express how *they* relate to God. And when our services reflect the beliefs that people hold today about Judaism, and God, and their own lives, and put these into new, beautiful words.

———————

Rabbi Samuel M. Cohon is the founding rabbi of Congregation Beit Simcha in Tucson, Arizona. Prior to rabbinic ordination at HUC-JIR, Rabbi Cohon was a commissioned cantor in the Cantors Assembly and a full-time *Hazzan* for seven years, serving Conservative and Reform congregations. He is co-author and editor of the *Shabbat Reflections Siddur* and *The Promise Haggadah*, and has recorded four professional albums of Jewish music and two albums of liturgy.

When I Was a Child
I Excommunicated Myself

—RABBI BOB ALPER

IN OUR REFORM SYNAGOGUE's youth services, we used *The Union Songster,* published by the Central Conference of American Rabbis, which explained authoritatively, "Prayer is talking to God," and "Let us try to hear God speaking to us. We can hear Him best when all is quiet."

So I was quiet, and I listened. I really listened. But I never heard God speaking to me. Maybe He talked with Joey on my right, or Sammy on my left, but never with me. Ever. I concluded that either I wasn't really Jewish, or that God just didn't want to talk to me.

Nearly seventy years later, nothing has changed. The liturgical vehicle of Reform Judaism may be meaningful to some. But, I am convinced, it excludes many.

A God We Can Believe In is a worthy and much-needed project. It presents a variety of God concepts that can offer, for some, revolutionary and even life-changing theological options. But for a significant percentage of Reform Jews, it is a project that will likely lead to disappointment and continued avoidance of Reform Jewish services. Simply stated, standard Reform Jewish liturgy does not meet the spiritual or intellectual needs of many people who seriously examine their own views of a deity. Thus, a book such as this is similar to presenting skis to a child who lives in Florida. A major change is needed before the gift becomes useful and valuable.

During my lifetime, from the explicit definition that "Prayer is talking to God" until today, Reform Jewish liturgists have worked with dedication and diligence to modernize our publications. Creating community liturgy for public worship is a daunting challenge. *The Union Prayer Book* (1940), uses Thee, Thou, and He when speaking of God. Only male patriarchs are cited. *Gates of Prayer* (1975), replaces Thee and Thou with You—while He and His remain. *Mishkan T'filah* (2007) drops He and His and adds the matriarchs to the patriarchs.

But the predominant underlying style was described by Rabbi Alvin Reines, z"l, Professor of Philosophy at The Hebrew Union College, as a form of theistic absolutism which may be termed "conversation theism,"[1] or speaking with God. And it marginalizes many readers by failing to uphold the theological freedom that ought to be reflected in every publication of the Reform Jewish movement.

Even more destructive is the prevailing theology reflected in the liturgy of Reform Judaism: theistic absolutism. Rabbi Reines described this as ". . . A concept of God according to which the word God refers to an omnipotent, omniscient, omnibenevolent, miracle-working being who created the human race and all the universe, who revealed commandments all women and men must obey, and who, depending on their obedience, dispenses to humankind supernatural rewards and punishments both in this world and in a hereafter."[2]

Consider these examples of the predominance of this exclusionary style of prayer and theology:

> "With a father's tender care Thou rememberest me every day and every hour."[3]
> "Eternal God...we need you as we need air to breathe."[4]
> "Blessed are You, *Adonai* our God . . . who bestows loving kindness . . ."[5]

Each edition included an increase in poetry and commentaries. But the central liturgy remained representative of one and only one Reform point of view, conversational theism/theistic absolutism. Despite earnest and creative cosmetic changes, other points of view are at best tangential, including those held by the vast numbers of atheists and agnostics who are part of, or wish to be part of, the Reform Jewish community.

Throughout my rabbinate I've imagined taking a theological survey of those sitting in the pews. I wanted to pause after reading, for example,

1. Reines, *Shabbath As A State of Being*, 37.
2. Reines, *Polydoxy*, 56.
3. Central Conference, *Union Prayer Book*, 35.
4. Stern, *Gates of Prayer*, 240.
5. Frishman, *Mishkan T'filah*, 166.

"You are our Sovereign; delivering us from the hand of oppressors, saving us from the fists of tyrants, doing wonders without number."[6] I would then pose two questions, and ask for a show of hands. How many of you actually speak with God? And are the words we just read true and meaningful for you? Although I would never ask for such personal revelations in a public forum, in a different way I have posed that very question many hundreds of times. The results have been astonishing.

Since the beginning of my rabbinate in 1972, I have given every bride and groom copies of two very different wedding ceremonies. One was a xerox of a CCAR *Rabbi's Manual* ceremony that offers words such as, "O God, supremely blessed, in might and glory, guide and bless this bridegroom and bride."[7] The other, a ceremony published by The Institute of Creative Judaism, begins, "Blessed are you who have come here in the name of love; in the spirit of love, we bless you." [8]

The CCAR wedding ceremony is God-centered with conversational theism and theistic absolutism throughout. In contrast, the I.C.J. ceremony implies, but does not mention, a divinity.

And of the more than six hundred couples to whom I offered the choice, not one, not a single solitary couple, chose the *Rabbi's Manual* ceremony. Never.

My selection of funeral readings drew similar reactions.

The *Rabbi's Manual* funeral services begin with "I have set the Eternal always before me. God is at my side."[9] I have never used those words. Rather, I usually begin with, "We have gathered together to share in a great sorrow, for every person in this room has learned again the meaning of loss."[10] No mention of a highly defined deity. Yet never has a mourner noticed anything unusual, commenting instead that they felt comfortable and comforted by the readings I chose.

Presenting Reform Jews with creative God concepts appropriate for our era can be revolutionary and life-enhancing. The challenge is, how does a community truly affirm such a diversity of liberal theologies? How can we avoid forcing people to sit in the synagogue—if they come at all—and hear and recite words they fundamentally do not believe?

6. Stern, *Gates of Repentance*, 57.

7. Central Conference, *Rabbi's Manual*, 35.

8. Polydox Institute, "Wedding Ceremony," line 1.

9. Plaut, *Rabbi's Manual*, 111.

10. Source unknown. Possibly original by author.

Rabbi Reines understood this destructive dilemma. He reminded us that in contrast to science, religion deals with issues beyond empirical proof, such as the definition of God and the nature of an afterlife. The very idea of ortho-doxy means, illogically, "the true opinion." If an opinion is true, it is no longer an opinion but is a verifiable fact. Orthodoxy's opposite is Polydoxy,[11] meaning "many opinions," a word that correctly describes the variety of theological opinions affirmed in the liberal Jewish community. A project to supply people with a variety of God definitions is totally consistent with the options open to the Polydox community. But absent a needed shift to an appropriate vehicle for communal prayer, the value of Reform Jewish community gatherings will continue to diminish.[12]

This concept is best described by a story told by the legendary journalist Harry Golden. When Golden's lifelong atheist father was elderly, he began attending synagogue daily. Asked why, he explained, "Everyone goes to synagogue for different reasons. Garfinkle goes to talk to God. I go to talk to Garfinkle." Like the elder Mr. Golden, many liberal Jews who still go to synagogue do so for the music, or the sermon, to talk to Garfinkle, or similar reasons. But most do not go to talk to God.

The reason so many liberal Jews do not find personal value in communal prayer is the way the specific theology espoused excludes them from feeling authentically involved. "Prayer is talking to God," I was told as a child. It is, to me, an exclusionary concept that continues to dominate and makes meaningless to me Reform Judaism's official liturgical face.

Rabbi Reines writes, depressingly but accurately, "To the objective observer, there can be little question that the traditional beliefs and rituals of the prevailing Jewish religious institutions are regarded by the majority of

---

11. Polydox Institute, "The Term Polydoxy," para 1.

12. Polydox Institute, "Questions and Answers." What is the essential characteristic of the Polydox liturgy or services? In order to serve the Polydox community, services have been produced whose essential characteristic is that they are theologically open, that is, non creedal and undogmatic. In a Polydox community, every person has the right to her or his own theological beliefs. Thus services intended for the general Polydox community must be theologically open so that persons with different theological views can participate with integrity and authenticity in the same service. In the case of ordinary services, where creedal and dogmatic language that expresses one particular theological view is employed, those present at the service who subscribe to other views must either exclude themselves from the service by remaining quiet, or mouth language whose meaning they consider untrue. In a Polydoxy, forced exclusion of a person from a community religious service by the use of creedal and dogmatic language is an infringement of the person's rights and a fundamental violation of the Covenant of Freedom.

Reform Jews as untrue or irrelevant. Increasing numbers of religiously unaffiliated Jews, temples and synagogues, deserted as they go about routine ceremonial functions, all testify to this fact."[13]

———————

The solution, the proper, effective, and meaningful form of prayer for a polydox Jewish community, is what Rabbi Reines termed "equivocal liturgy." Equivocal means equi-vocal, or giving equal voice to the many theological positions affirmed within liberal Judaism.

A simple example: When a theistic absolutist who engages God in conversation and a person who posits God as the first cause who does not interfere in human life sit together and read, "Thank you God for this splendid day," the first congregant feels theologically validated and moved, while the second likely feels excluded and uncomfortable. But if the prayer were changed to the equivocal, "We are thankful for this splendid day," both individuals can derive, in different ways, meaning and inspiration from the very same words.[14]

Consider the enduring popularity of Eccl 3:1–8: "A season is set for everything. . . " Polydox. Equivocal. Theologically neutral. Or Rabbi Alvin Fine, "Birth is a beginning and death a destination; but life is a journey. . ." Again, Polydox. Equivocal. Theologically neutral.

The Polydoxy.org website offers a host of polydox, equivocal holiday, and life cycle services (some of which I wrote or co-wrote) appropriate and meaningful for everyone in the Reform Jewish community, from atheists like Harry Golden's father to theistic absolutists.

Rabbi Reines courageously addressed *Shabbat* as well, substituting the concept of *Shabbat* as a state of being for the traditional sunset to sunset model. To be candid, during my years serving congregations I was tasked with promoting the marvelous values of *Shabbat* while, in my own life, *Shabbat* was the hardest part of the week. It was the evening and day on

13. Reines, *Shabbath As A State of Being*, 37.

14. Polydox Institute, "Questions and Answers." Non creedal and undogmatic services are produced by writing the liturgy of the service in "multivalent" (equivocal) language. Multivalent language is a technical term, and means language that espouses no single theological creed or dogma. Thus multivalent services do not express a particular theological viewpoint. Rather, they use language as a vehicle to communicate information and inspiration in such a manner that the participant is free to fill creatively her or his mind and heart with whatever theological content is desired.

which my performance was judged, my interactions with congregants critical, and my attention to details central. *Shabbat*: the sublime day of rest. Really, rabbi?

Dr. Reines recognized that a time-bound *Shabbat* can be meaningful for some, including those who strive to make the day of *Shabbat* into what it promises.[15] But for so many for whom our complex lives get in the way, including rabbis whose professions center on *Shabbat*, he proposed recognition of *Shabbat* as a state of being. Simply put, if Tuesday afternoon turns out to be an anxiety-free time of relaxation and peacefulness, one should not simply enjoy it but, more importantly, recognize it as holy. This delightful state of being is worthy of being identified as *Shabbat*.

Both equivocal liturgy and observing *Shabbat* as a state of being would have deeply enhanced my spiritual life. But these honest, logical, and courageous steps require a community. Thus far I have not found one. Perhaps someday Reform Judaism will break free of the tyranny of theistic absolutism, replacing the liturgy that does not speak to many, and has been abandoned by those who have left behind empty pews.

Rabbi Bob Alper served congregations in Buffalo and Philadelphia for fourteen years and continued to conduct High Holy services in Philadelphia for another thirty-four years. He has been a full-time stand-up comic since 1988 and is the author of three books, two CDs, and a DVD. He was ordained by the Hebrew Union College and earned a Doctor of Ministry degree from The Princeton Theological Seminary.

15. Reines, *Shabbath As A State of Being*, 38.

In Search of the Divine

—Rabbi Seymour Prystowsky

HAVING BEEN RAISED IN an Orthodox home and having been schooled mostly in *yeshiva*, I was taught the basic beliefs of traditional Judaism. They included the belief that God exists as a supernatural deity; that we do not have absolute freedom of will; that God can and does intervene in our lives; that God listens and responds to prayer; that God can suspend natural law; and that God rewards the righteous and punishes the wicked.

I remember in one of my classes raising the question of God having hardened Pharaoh's heart. It seemed to indicate that even though the Pharaoh permitted the Children of Israel to leave Egypt, God changed Pharaoh's mind. Why then blame Pharaoh for not letting the people go? The *yeshiva* teacher silenced me for raising what he considered to be a heretical question.

On another occasion, I asked the teacher how the Israelites crossed the Sea of Reeds as the Egyptians were pursuing them. The text in the Torah says that God split the sea for the Israelites enabling them to walk on dry land, an example of natural law being suspended. I questioned, "How can God suspend his own laws of nature?" I was called an *Apikoros* (irreverent, a non-believer) and my *rebbe* reprimanded me for questioning God's ability to do anything he wanted to.

These experiences affected my life significantly. I realized that I had to find answers to my religious questions elsewhere.

As I grew older, I rejected the beliefs in which I had been indoctrinated. I could no longer affirm that an outside power intervened in our lives. We humans, through our cruelty and indifference, are responsible for the evils of the world. If a person is to be accountable for his deeds, like the

Pharaoh, he must have freedom of will. We are not puppets whose strings are pulled by an outside force. Nor is our life predetermined by a supernatural deity. If each individual has freedom of will, it means that natural law cannot be suspended by God. God is not a tooth fairy, and cannot be made into one, not by ritual, and not by prayer.

David Hume put it bluntly: "Epicurus's old questions are still unanswered: Is he (God) willing to prevent evil, but not able? Then he is impotent. Is he able, but not willing? Then he is malevolent. Is he both able and willing? Then whence evil?"[1] As my teacher, Dr. Henry Slonimsky, z"l, who introduced me to this thought, often said, "Either God wants to intervene but is not able to, or God is able to intervene and does not want to."

Many of us believe the former, that God is not able to. Regardless of what view we have of God—a Creator, a Power, an Idea, or an Ideal, the *Shoah* has forced us to confront the issue of innocent suffering. The question of God's absence during those horrendous years has not been answered satisfactorily. One prominent Orthodox rabbi, Walter Wurzburger, has written often on this subject. He stated that, ". . . It makes perfect sense to argue that from a divine perspective all evil must be necessary, even if, from our limited understanding, we cannot fathom the reason for it's a necessity"[2] [And] all we can do is confront the mystery of God's involvement in the history of the people which he elected for his service."[3] In other words, God chose to absent himself but we don't know why.

I find that view problematic. The truth is that our prophets and sages often brought God before the bar of history. And when I hear that millions of innocent souls were slaughtered, the answer that God must have had a mysterious reason for not having intervened is utterly unacceptable. Besides, the fact remains that God did not intervene. And that has to be factored into one's theology.

After the *Shoah*, Arthur Cohen wrote, "The question is not how can God abide evil in the world, but how can God be affirmed meaningfully in a world where evil enjoys such dominion[4]He concludes that the God who emerges is not the god of traditional theology. This strongly suggests that God can no longer be the God of traditional prayer books. And I daresay that this God cannot be the God of our Reform prayer books either.

1. Hume, *Dialogue*, 63.
2. Wurzburger, *Ethics*, 14.
3. Wurzburger, *Theological and Philosophical Responses*, 32.
4. Cohen, *Tremendum*, 34.

Many of us, like Arthur Cohen, do not believe that God intervenes in our lives in order to alter the course of human events. This has serious implications for our liturgy. It means that all the prayers that petition God to intercede in our lives, all the prayers that express our gratitude to God for active participation in our lives, and all the prayers that refer to God as *El Rahum v'Hanun* (God of mercy and compassion), do not express our beliefs.

The High Holydays present special challenges. The *Unetaneh Tokef* prayer is based on the belief that God examines our behavior over the past year on *Rosh Hashanah* and decides who shall live and who shall die before sealing the decision on *Yom Kippur*. God's merciful intervention, of course, is sought. This should not be a part of the liturgy we hope to create.

Similarly, *Avinu Malkenu* pictures God as controlling our lives. The prayer petitions God to inscribe us in the Book of Life, a request I do not believe God can grant.

Today's worship services are structurally and textually geared towards worshiping a God who is the omnipotent, omniscient, compassionate intervening deity, who listens and hears our petitions, praises, and thanks, and responds to them. This encourages the belief in miracles, not as the incredible realities we experience every day, but as supernatural acts of intervention.

The Jewish journey to behold the Divine presence began with a sacrificial system. In biblical times it was considered authentic Judaism. After the destruction of the Second Temple, the rabbis introduced the second stage in our religious development: communal prayer addressed to a supernatural intervening deity. This has been the norm for the past two thousand years. I am suggesting that this practice give way to stage three: gatherings of Jewish people on weekdays, *Shabbat*, festivals, and High Holy Days, to study, sing, reflect, meditate, chant, and recite prayers and mantras that give hope, a sense of community, and especially, a sense of holiness. Such services should inspire, educate, comfort, and unite us as a people. They should not seek intervention from a personal God but rather emphasize our responsibilities as individuals and the potential of humankind.

Services, therefore, should not consist of words and songs that compromise our spiritual or intellectual integrity. They should, however, provide us with words and songs that inspire us with courage and hope without having to compromise our beliefs. That will strengthen us as we participate in these new services.

I stress hope because to live without hope is to live in despair. And despair is a cardinal sin in Judaism. It is to succumb to the darkness that threatens us. Our belief is that tomorrow can be better than today and that we can bring it about, not by petitioning a God to intervene, but by energizing ourselves to work together to achieve our goal. It is our belief that God needs us to act, that God wants us to act, and that God depends upon us to act. Ultimately, we are the agents of the Divine.

Having stated all of the above, I still stand in awe before the mysteries of the universe, which reveal daily the extraordinary order of the cosmos and the incredible complexity of existence. I place my faith in further discoveries that encourage me to continue my journey in seeking a Divine Presence.

───────────

Rabbi Seymour Prystowsky was ordained as a rabbi by the Hebrew Union College—Jewish Institute of Religion, New York, in 1961. After serving two years as a chaplain in the US Army, he came to Congregation Or Ami, a Reform synagogue in Lafayette Hill, PA, and served as the spiritual leader there for thirty-eight years. He is now Rabbi Emeritus. He earned a Ph.D. from Dropsie University and holds certification as a family therapist from the Eastern Pennsylvania Psychiatric Institute in Philadelphia.

Language for the High Holydays

—RABBI NEIL COMESS-DANIELS

LIKE MANY OF US, my journey into the many layers of meaning behind various prayer translations in the *siddur* (prayer book), be it Reform, Conservative, or Orthodox, began pretty early in my life, shortly after I became *Bar Mitzvah*. At the time, my family belonged to a Conservative congregation. One Saturday morning, I sat with my peers while another of our cohort went through his service. Having learned/memorized my prayers, I decided to look at the English translation of what I was reciting in Hebrew. I recall saying clearly and definitively to myself, "If this is what this prayer means, I don't believe it." I remember the English translation grating against my theology—such as it was at the time. It felt awful. I was angry, disappointed, and although I didn't fully understand it, betrayed. Why hadn't anyone sat down with me and told me the truth? At least we could have a conversation.

It turned out not to be a case of early adolescent rebellion. The struggle stayed with me. I became accustomed to it though, assuming there was no alternative. I could "get by" attending a service and participating. I loved the melodies, so I just focused on the music. That worked for about two and a half years until an older friend and mentor, who was somewhat of a jazz piano prodigy, was invited to entertain troops in Viet Nam. We were all so proud of him and in awe of this unique opportunity. While there, he was killed in an ambush. That ended any prayer for me for quite a while. The betrayal I felt years before came home to roost. Now I knew precisely what that betrayal was all about.

After my first year of college, I accepted a position as a counselor at a Jewish summer camp. Even though I was in theological limbo and angry at Judaism for not helping me process my friend's tragic death, I still identified as a Jew, and, as a result, I figured I could do the job. I never anticipated that my "kids" would have the same questions about The War and the world as I did. I committed myself not to answer their questions. Instead, I gave them what I wanted those many years before—a conversation. I fell in love with engaging with others in that truthful and direct way. That new love for a values clarification approach to teaching, coupled with the music I learned at camp (for prayers that STILL troubled me), formed part of the internal catalyst that led me to rabbinical school.

Along the path of my rabbinic career, my theology kept changing and growing. I began tugging on the words of prayers in Hebrew to mold and nuance translations in English that truly reflected what I believed (or *wanted to believe*) the Hebrew original was trying to communicate. Some years ago, those struggles first crystallized for me in a translation for the *Sh'ma*. Even though the *Sh'ma* was initially a declaration by Moses to our ancient ancestors, we employ these words as a prayer. Usually rendered as "Hear, O Israel, the Lord our God, the Lord is One." The current Reform prayer book, *Mishkan T'filah*, updates it to "Listen, Israel, *Adonai* is our God, *Adonai* is One!" Here's my tug:

"Hear this, Israel, the Unity-of-All is God; Everything is One."[1]

People are often a bit stunned by such a translation that uses different epithets and hyphen-linked phrases to describe the possibility of the Divine. That's good. Such a translation, especially when compared to the conventional one, is designed to generate a double-take. My liturgy professor at Hebrew Union College was (and still is) Rabbi Dr. Larry Hoffman. Recently, he described Judaism as "a conversation," precisely what I yearned for when I was young. It's what we all need now and into the future. After all, we are not "Reform*ed*" Judaism. The reforming didn't finish—and it should never conclude. The discussion continues.

A significant part of the conversation is the process of constantly striving for more creative, theologically inclusive, and challenging translations and understandings of our prayers. Our prayers are part of our Jewish sociological glue. However, this Jewish adhesive was always silicone-like and malleable, not super glue. Attempting to preserve and protect Judaism from the vicissitudes of history, the Talmudic practice of laying commentary upon commentary became ossified within some approaches to our legal and interpretative tradition. Commentaries and interpretations

1. © Neil Comess-Daniels

are kept within strict parameters. It's the wrong strategy. Judaism, as we have "done" it, was always an organic process. It is the responsibility of the Reform movement to ensure that it stays that way.

––––––––––

We say the *Sh'ma* evening and morning all year long. What about prayers and prayerful expressions unique to specific times of the year, like the High Holy Days? We fill these ten days with moments of high emotion and deeply emotional melodies. The evening service of *Rosh Hashanah* begins in that mode with a prayer called *Hineni*. (The *Hineni* occurs during the *Musaf* service in traditional *mahzorim*.) Only the cantor or lead facilitator recites *Hineni*. The first few words express the essence of the prayer:

> "*Hineni*—Here I am, impoverished in deeds and merit. Nevertheless, I have come before You, God, to plead on behalf of Your people Israel.

In other words, the cantor, praying on behalf of the congregation, declares him/herself unequal to the task. The phrase "I have come before You, God. . ." is essential for us to parse. That image, which essentially portrays God holding court like a monarch with petitioners coming before the throne, is seductive—and dangerous. Unfortunately, millions of Jews (and non-Jews) took these images literally over the centuries rather than metaphorically. A verbatim understanding was never the intent. The High Holy Day liturgy is replete with such imagery. Some of Judaism's most luminous rabbis railed against these images and cautioned us not to be seduced by them.

Perhaps the most famous example of these warnings is that of Moses Maimonides, the Rambam. In his text, the *Guide for the Perplexed*, he teaches forcefully about anthropomorphism, the employing of human attributes to describe God:

> "You, no doubt, know the Talmudical saying, which includes in itself all the various kinds of interpretation connected with our subject [anthropomorphism]. It runs thus: "The Torah speaks according to the language of man," that is to say, expressions, which can easily be comprehended and understood by all, are applied to the Creator. Hence the description of God by attributes implying corporeality in order to express His existence: because the multitude of people do not easily conceive existence unless in

connection with a body, and that which is not a body nor connected with a body has for them no existence."[2]

These statements are direct and harsh. Rambam essentially disqualifies those who have a belief about God that includes any connection with anything physical. In another of his works, the *Mishneh Torah*, he lists five categories of those who *do not* believe. The third category is:

"Those who say that there is One Lord; but that He is corporeal and has a form."[3]

Even in his famous Thirteen Principles of Faith, he insists upon a theology that God is formless, "God is incorporeal–without a body." This is elaborated in his *Mishneh Torah*.[4]

Another outstanding Sephardic commentator, Moses Cordovero, is much more direct and demeaning to those who anthropomorphize God:

A [spiritually] impoverished person (עָנִי—*ani*) thinks that God is an old man with white hair, sitting on a wondrous throne of fire that glitters with countless sparks, as it is written:
"And the Ancient of Days (God) took His seat. His garment was like white snow, And the hair of His head was like lamb's wool. His throne was tongues of flame." (Dan 7:9) Imagining this and similar fantasies, the fool corporealizes God. He falls into one of the traps that destroy faith. His awe of God is limited by his imagination. But if you are enlightened, you know God's oneness. You know that the Divine is devoid of bodily categories—these can never be applied to God.[5]

When I first began my rabbinic studies, I learned two important points about the Hebrew word for prayer, *tefillah*—תפילה. The first is that the primary meaning of the root of the word, PaLaL—פ-ל-ל, is not "to pray," but rather "to judge." The other crucial feature of the term *tefillah* is that its infinitive form, *l'hit-Pa-LeiL* is "reflexive." This "reflexivity" means the energy flow of the judgment/prayer goes out into the "Everythingness" of the Universe and *turns around*, like a boomerang, whence it came. Putting together the core meaning of *tefillah* as "judgment" and the reflexive character of the word itself creates a beautiful metaphor of prayer as "self-judgment." When we pray, we are not "judged" by some outside force or

2. *Guide for the Perplexed* I:26.1.
3. *Mishneh Torah: Hilhot Teshuvah*, 3:7.
4. *Mishneh Torah: Hilhot Y'sodei haTorah*, 1:9.
5. *Or Ne'erav* II:2.3.

Divinity. Instead, we judge *ourselves*, our state of mind, emotions, sincerity, focus, actions, commitment. The poetry of these images indicates that we must hear, respond to, or answer our prayers. Prayer is a taking on of responsibility, not a letting go.

During *Rosh Hashanah* and *Yom Kippur,* when we face a bombardment of kingly and royal court images, significant challenges arise when we bring along notions of "Everythingness/the Oneness-of-All" and prayer as reflexive judgment. Several alternatives arise. We could:

- Throw our hands up in frustration and walk away
- Somehow "get along" by placing our focus on the melodies and/or the emotional impact of the ritual, ceremony, and traditions without allowing the literal meaning to bring a sense of dissonance
- Retool the words and translations in our minds
- Recognize it may be time to create revised and new liturgies that pray *with* Everything rather than *to* anything or anyone.

There's a gorgeous Chasidic idea that we are not separate from God trying to get closer. We are *within* God trying to understand the implications of being a small but significant part of Divinity. Hasidic thought also presents a viewpoint that not only is God's corporeality theologically oxymoronic, but the physical manifestation of Divinity via Creation also isn't necessary—a beautiful way to embrace the preciousness of our human existence. They say, "The world is God with clothes on." Our friend, Moses Cordovero, expresses it more lyrically:

> "The essence of divinity is found in every single thing—nothing but it exists. Since it causes every thing to be, no thing can live by anything else. It enlivens them; its existence exists in each existent. Do not attribute duality to God. Let God be solely God. If you suppose that *Ein Sof* emanates until a certain point and that from that point on is outside of it, you have dualized. Realize, rather, that *Ein Sof* exists in each existent. Do not say, "This is a stone and not God." Rather, all existence is God, and the stone is a thing pervaded by divinity."[6]

Instead of *wishing* that our prayers reflected these perspectives, they should. They must. Our Reform movement's most recent *Mahzor* (High Holy Day prayer book), *Mishkan HaNefesh,* makes some attempts to

---

6. Cordovero, *Shi'ur Qomah,* 154.

address the overwhelming presence of anthropomorphic depictions of God in Jewish literature and liturgy. For example, it "neutralizes" the gender of God by repeating the word God or substituting *Adonai* for He/His/Him. The text also uses "Sovereign" rather than "King."

These efforts are praiseworthy, but they don't go far enough. When we parse the word *Adonai* and realize that it's not a name but rather a descriptive term for God that translates as "All-Being," then actually employing epithets like All-Being, Everything, Oneness, and Unity-of-All honestly say what many of us feel.

Of course, some High Holy Day phraseology cannot be fixed by merely replacing the word God with alternative words and phrases. These pieces go deep into a dualistic viewpoint about God that we can only attend to by wrestling with the structural issues in the liturgy itself and changing what we say.

One such prayer is *B'Rosh Hashanah*. Traditionally, we say:

> On *Rosh Hashanah* this is written; on the Fast of *Yom Kippur* this is sealed:
>> How many will pass away from this world,
>> how many will be born into it;
>> who will live and who will die;
>> who will reach the ripeness of age,
>> who will be taken before their time;
>> who by fire and who by water;
>> who by war and who by beast;
>> who by famine and who by drought;
>> who by earthquake and who by plague;
>> who by strangling and who by stoning;
>> who will rest and who will wander;
>> who will be tranquil and who will be troubled;
>> who will be calm and who tormented;
>> who will live in poverty and who in prosperity;
>> who will be humbled and who exalted —[7]

With an acceptance of a non-dual theology, the elimination of monarchical imagery, using prayer as an opportunity to pray with Everything, and accepting responsibility within Divinity, my version comes out as a set of challenges, instead of Karmic questions:

> Since we know not the number of our days as complex humans,
> and before we become part of the earth and flow into other forms,

7. Goldberg, *Mishkan HaNefesh: Yom Kippur*, 212.

perhaps it is better *to live* until we cannot, and better to ask *these* questions *about ourselves* and our year:

Who will live like a fire that warms and welcomes others in from the cold?

Who will live like water, giving and sharing life and love?

Who will live with a hunger for helping, bringing sustenance to those who have none?

Who will shake the foundations of a stale status quo and be an earthquake for freedom so that those who remain trapped within roles of unfulfillment and inequality might be released?

Who shall live with creative restlessness, bringing rest, safety, and shelter to those who have no rest, who are fleeing injustice, violence, and natural calamity?

Who shall live with a richness of spirit, sharing their prosperity whose lives, souls, bodies, and minds are impoverished?[8]

Some prayers are so inviolable and laden with communal and individual symbolism, we dare not touch a word or a letter. *Kol Nidre* is such a prayer. A mythological entity whose origins are shrouded in mystery, *Kol Nidre* is of such import to so many, we should leave the original text alone. *Kol Nidre* was a challenge to even the most traditionally established Jewish perspective because it is a declaration of liability for unfulfilled vows. There were several attempts to change the wording or the haunting melody (also of mysterious origins). The communal pushback was tsunamic.

What can we do in the case of sacrosanct prayer like *Kol Nidre* if we realize that it is too crucial a thread in our Jewish cultural tapestry that it cannot or should not change? We can create a buffer for it in the *Mahzor* before or after the prayer.

Here, I offer my own. In it, I try to reflect a taking on of responsibility rather than a release from it. The reading alludes to the reflexive nature of prayer in describing the cyclical nature of the year—three hundred sixty-four days on either side of *Yom Kippur*. In the *Machzor* I created with my synagogue, we placed these words after *Kol Nidre*:

On this awesome evening
We confess our humanity to ourselves
within the Oneness-of-All,
and in the presence of our community.
We often become frustrated, angry with who we are,
furious at our failings.

8. © Neil Comess-Daniels

Other times we are not angry enough.
We delude ourselves by diluting our potential.
This year we will try once again
To vow with sincerity.
We have only one day to review
the three-hundred and sixty-four that have preceded it.
And that same day in which to
turn ourselves toward the three-hundred and sixty-four
that will follow.
We are now at that day's beginning.
Many words, dreams, songs, and hopes later
we will be at its end.
We pray that between two settings of the sun,
our sincerity will rise.

I leave you with an introduction I wrote and set to music as a preface to *Avinu Malkeinu*, another prayer of mythological stature in Jewish culture. Its title comes from the first phrase of every couplet, *Avinu Malkeinu*, Our Father, Our King—a limited, limiting, gender insensitive, and ominous image. For this piece, I strung together alternative epithets for the Divine that reflect the approach discussed above:

BREATH-OF-ALL
Filling-All-Worlds
Unknown-and-Known
Embracing-All-Spheres
Above-Below
Nothing-Else-Is-
Was-or-Will Be
Ever-Deep-Pool
Fountain-Flow
Presence-in-All
Source-of-Life
Darkness-of-Darkness
Lights-of-Light
Always-Beginning
Only-One-Soul
Never-an-End
Breath-of-All[9]

9. © Neil Comess-Daniels

And so, the work and conversation continue. May we know many blessings within the Oneness-of-All, pray with All, and may every inhale of the Breath-of-Life inspire us to be instruments for love and peace.

———————

Rabbi Neil Comess-Daniels is the Rabbi Emeritus of Beth Shir Shalom, the progressive Reform synagogue in Santa Monica/West Los Angeles (after twenty-nine years). He received his rabbinic ordination at Hebrew Union College–Jewish Institute of religion in 1979 and his Doctor of Divinity degree in 2004. He is the recipient of many local honors, including the Giants of Justice Award from Clergy and Laity United for Economic Justice and the Community Peace Award from the Muslim Public Affairs Council. His first album of music for children and their families, *On This Day and All The Time,* is available on iTunes.

Music in Non-Theistic Worship

—Rabbi Jeffrey B. Stiffman

Music touches our emotions in ways that spoken words do not. Music can move the worshiper to develop understanding, concern, enthusiasm, and pride. Music is essential to the Jewish worship service, adding emotion, memory, and historical connection to the overall experience.

Yet in traditional theistic worship, many prayers that have been set to music express ideas, philosophy, or theology that are unacceptable to nontheists. How can we preserve the essential components that music adds without compromising our intellectual or spiritual integrity?

MUSICAL WORSHIP IS EVER-EVOLVING

Music has played an important role in worship throughout history. Traditional prayers have been chanted or sung, in a great diversity of modes and melodies, since Biblical times. Over the centuries, various communities and countries developed their own chants and melodies. One could often tell a Jewish person's origin city by the tones of his prayers. Musical diversity continues to this day, in every Jewish stream.

A musical revolution began in the nineteenth century, at the time of the "Enlightenment" in Judaism. The liberal (Reform, Positive-Historical, and other) movements in Europe wished to create more modern and aesthetic services. They felt that the traditional "Oriental chant" was not pleasing to the contemporary ear and began to incorporate newer musical forms and melodies into synagogue worship. Musical reform in Europe included melodies led by cantors, accompanied by organs, mixed choirs, and other ensembles. Some cantors set their prayers to operatic arias while others copied popular tunes. The classical-sounding music of composers such as Louis Lewandowski, Solomon Sulzer, and others was widely admired. Some congregations took tunes from non-Jewish sources and adapted them to Jewish settings. The Western European Reformers, especially, admired the singing of hymns in Christian worship, and this resulted in the publication of the first Jewish hymnals.

Liberal European Jews who migrated to North America brought these musical traditions with them. The melodies of the German and Austrian Reform synagogues became the musical standard of American Reform congregations in the nineteenth and twentieth centuries. During this period, there was often a Hymnal or Songster in the pew alongside the prayerbook. The Reform *Union Hymnal* included such selections as "Onward Brothers, March Still Onward," set to a theme from Beethoven's Ninth Symphony with words by Havelock Ellis. It was even included in later Christian hymnals!

Three American Jewish movements pioneered musical worship creativity: Reform Judaism, Reconstructionist Judaism, and Humanistic Judaism. Reform *siddurim* have reflected major theological changes, in one case offering a completely non-theistic *Shabbat* evening service in *Gates of Prayer* (1975). The Reconstructionist movement adopted the theology of its founder Mordecai Kaplan and deleted all references to God having "chosen our people," emphasizing instead that it is people who choose God. The Humanistic Jewish movement has rewritten the liturgy to eliminate any and all traditional references to a controlling Deity.

ELIMINATE, OBFUSCATE, REWRITE OR REINTERPRET

Eliminate

One way to deal with an intellectually offensive prayer is to simply remove it from the movement's *siddur* or *mahzor*. The Reform movement did this frequently in the nineteenth century, eliminating prayers calling for the rebuilding of the Jerusalem Temple, the reestablishment of the priesthood, and the reinstatement of sacrificial offerings. Also deemed incompatible with modernity was the belief in a personal messiah. Other liberal Jewish movements have rewritten *siddurim* to be congruous with their own particular teachings. Yet there remains an emotional barrier to removing some of the most revered prayers. How many times have we heard Jews complain when one of their cherished prayers or songs is no longer used?

Obfuscate

Another way to deal with theological dissonance was obfuscation. Instead of speaking the words in English, they were sung only in the original Hebrew or Aramaic. Since most worshipers do not have enough knowledge of the original to translate, it avoided having to confront the plain meaning of the words themselves.

Rewrite or Reinterpret

The *Kol Nidre*, chanted at the beginning of the *Yom Kippur* evening service, is the most prominent example of the power of melody to trump dogma. It is actually not a prayer, but a legal document allowing an individual to escape punishment for unfulfilled promises made to God. Though it is entirely anachronistic and not binding, many Jews feel that it is not *Yom Kippur* unless *Kol Nidre* is chanted. In fact, the entire *Yom Kippur* evening service is often referred to as the "*Kol Nidre* Service." However, few people, aside from scholars and rabbis, have thought seriously about the words of *Kol Nidre* in English.

As far back as Gaonic times, Rabbis debated whether or not to eliminate it.[1] Early Reform Judaism did eliminate it from its prayer books. Rabbi Leo Stern wrote alternative words and set them to the melody, "*O Tag des Herrn!*—O Day of the Lord" (1840). Early Reform prayerbooks in North America excluded *Kol Nidre* altogether, often substituting an English translation of Stern's German reading. But they kept the music.

Kol Nidre was not officially restored to Reform Jewish High Holyday prayer until the publication of *Gates of Repentance* in 1978. It was not done because of the words, but because of the emotional pull of the music. Its drama and emotion were too deeply embedded in Jewish consciousness for worshippers to discard. One can stand and be touched by the haunting and moving melody that gives *Yom Kippur* much of its emotional resonance.

Among Reconstructionist Jews, *Kol Nidre* was briefly omitted from the official liturgy but was subsequently restored with a revised text. It

---

1. Jacobs et al., *Kol Nidre*, para. 12.

limited its application to those vows that operated "to estrange ourselves from those who have offended us" or "to give pain to those who have angered us." The melody remained.

The most glaring example of cognitive dissonance is exhibited by *Kol Nidre*'s presence in Humanistic Jewish worship. The Birmingham Temple, in Birmingham, Michigan, is the home of Humanistic Judaism, its "Mother Church," so to speak. Humanistic Judaism officially eliminates worship of a Divine God, going so far as to substitute the word *Adam*—meaning Human—on the wall where an ark would stand in most synagogues. The movement has created worship services that are largely rational in their approach to the universe.

One would not think that such services would include *Kol Nidre*, but some Rabbis proceeded to introduce that very prayer as a link with the past and with Jews around the world, because of its haunting melody. Emotion trumped intellectuality.

USING NON-THEISTIC SONG TEXTS

There are many songs and texts that do not create issues for the non-theistic worshiper. Biblical songs such as *Hinay Mah Tov* and *Dodi Li* can be sung alongside modern ones such as *Bim Bam, Hevenu Shalom Alehem,* and Hasidic *nigunim*. All of these can add depth and emotion to the worship experience. The many melodies that highlight Jewish themes such as togetherness, unity, love, *Shabbat*, and peace can likewise be sung without intellectual compromise.

DEVELOPING A NEW MUSICAL GENRE IN NORTH AMERICA

The number of contemporary composers of Jewish music, who include many non-theistic songwriters, is growing. Some were young song leaders at camps and youth conclaves who continue to compose as adults. National gatherings such as *Hava Nashira* in Illinois and the "Song Leader's Boot Camp" in Missouri attract hundreds of Jewish music creators each year. Jewish Rock Radio is a source of fun and inspiration for thousands of Jews. Much of this music has found its way into synagogue worship.

IN ISRAEL

Mordecai Kaplan, the founder of Reconstructionist Judaism, believed in the concept of "Judaism As a Civilization." He foresaw a society in which liturgical and artistic creativity would be free to thrive unbound by traditional strictures. The synagogue and synagogue school would become but one part of a broader Jewish life. This vision of liturgical creativity has been realized in the State of Israel, where Hebrew language, Jewish thought, Jewish arts, and Jewish music flourish and thrive.

Much of Israeli popular and folk music includes the Jewish theme of hope for the future. One of the most famous of these songs is *Od Yavo Shalom Aleinu— Salaam* written by Mosh Ben-Ari. He wrote it for his band *Sheva*, which is comprised of both Jews and Arabs. It incorporates the words for peace in both Hebrew and Arabic—*shalom* and *salaam*. Music such as this links Jews around the world in hopes for peace with their Arab neighbors. It is heard increasingly in both formal and informal worship services. The Israeli influence upon modern Jewish music is immeasurable, and a rich source for those for whom traditional theology is no longer acceptable.

A CHALLENGE AND ITS REWARDS

The challenge of enriching non-theistic worship with musical emotion continues. I believe that adapting Jewish music to tradition and creating new forms of it can enrich our spiritual lives without violating our beliefs. Drawing from our history, our diversity, and the creativity of our generation, we can engage hearts and minds in new ways, enhancing the Jewish experience with artistry, integrity, and joy.

Rabbi Jeffrey B. Stiffman, Ph.D., DD, is Rabbi Emeritus of Congregation Shaare Emeth in St. Louis, Missouri. As a student, he was Chapel Organist and Choir Director on the Cincinnati campus of the Hebrew Union College.

Crowns—The Tension Between *Pshat* and *Drash*

—Rabbi Philip Graubart

WHAT DOES RABBI AKIVA believe? It's an important question; he was tortured to death because of his beliefs. Yet in rabbinic sources, he says very little about God. Instead, he manifests a way of reading Torah, a hermeneutic, which becomes a surprisingly useful postmodern theology. In short, Akiva believes in *drash*, as opposed to *pshat*.

Pshat indicates the literal meaning of a text, the meaning we glean through context, grammar, vocabulary—the way most of us read most texts most of the time. *Drash*, on the other hand, suggests a wildly creative approach to reading, where meaning, based on a few hints, can warp off into all different directions. *Drash* turns a few verses about not boiling a kid in its mother's milk (Exod 23:19) into a complex system of separating meat and dairy. It takes the few *pshat* details we know about Abraham's life before God calls him and offers a rich portrait of a rebellious child smashing idols and looking for God. It transforms the Song of Songs from a collection of erotic love poems (the clear *pshat*) into a pious meditation on the relationship between God and the Jewish people. *Drash* reveals a hidden divine world below the surface and allows Judaism to change and grow. Akiva is its champion.

We see this most clearly by comparing Moses and Akiva in the following strange and beautiful Talmudic tale:

> Rab Judah said in the name of Rab, When Moses ascended on high he found the Holy One, blessed be He, engaged in affixing coronets to the letters.
>
> Said Moses, Lord of the Universe, Who delays you?

He answered, There will arise a man, at the end of many generations, Akiva b. Joseph by name, who will expound upon each
tittle heaps and heaps of laws. Lord of the Universe, said Moses;
permit me to see him. He replied, Turn thee round.

Moses went and sat down behind eight rows [and listened to
the discourses upon the law]. Not being able to follow their arguments he was ill at ease, but when they came to a certain subject
and the disciples said to the master, Whence do you know it?,
and the latter replied, It is a law given unto Moses at Sinai, he was
comforted.

Thereupon he returned to the Holy One, blessed be He, and
said, Lord of the Universe, Thou hast such a man and Thou givest
the Torah by me! He replied, Be silent, for such is My decree.

Then said Moses, Lord of the Universe, Thou hast shown me
his Torah, show me his reward. Turn thee round, said He; and
Moses turned around and saw them weighing out his flesh at the
market stalls. Lord of the Universe, cried Moses, such Torah, and
such a reward! He replied, Be silent, for such is My decree.[1]

Moses climbs Mt. Sinai to receive the Torah and bring it to his recently
liberated people. When he sees God adorning the letters, his first concern
is timing. What's the delay? he asks. From Moses' perspective, the Israelites need the law right now. Readers of the story, familiar with the Biblical
text, understand that the people are about to reject Moses and turn to the
Golden Calf. Moses senses or intuits the coming anarchy. He doesn't have
a moment to spare. The people need order, structure, commandments. But
God is wasting time, drawing crowns.

Moses here exhibits a *pshat* personality; he is only interested in the
literal meaning of the Torah's words. For Moses, the Torah is a tool he needs
to build social cohesion, as a constitution. He's got a job to do, and he'll do
it with the *pshat,* with the literal meaning. It wouldn't occur to the Moses in
our story to dig deeply for hidden meanings, to somehow discover "heaps
and heaps" of laws buried in a decoration. There's no time for creative reflection, and really, it's not necessary. The people, right now, need to learn
right and wrong, to honor their parents, to avoid theft, to worship the one
God. Why dive past the surface if the surface is all you need?

Akiva, on the other hand, leaves the *pshat* far behind. He teaches a
Torah that Moses, the first reader, doesn't recognize. But when his students wonder where Akiva got all this, he tells them it came to Moses at

1. b. Men. 29b.

Sinai. Akiva's majestic creativity, in other words, comes strictly through interpretation. He's not writing a new Torah. He's ceaselessly discovering new meanings in the old one. Akiva here exhibits a *drash* personality—a method of Torah study where you open your mind to the possibility of infinite interpretations. In the story, Akiva invents Torah study as a spiritual activity. He encounters God's infinite presence in the letters of the Torah, and in their decorations. God, for Akiva, means endless possibilities, bottomless interpretive opportunities. If Moses himself doesn't recognize Akiva's Torah, then Torah can go anywhere, mean anything. To believe in God is to believe in the infinite power of the text, along with the human individual's spiritual will to interpret, ask questions, find new meanings. No line of inquiry is ever closed off because everything is possible. "Turn it and turn it," as it says in *Pirke Avot*. "Everything is in it."[2]

Ironic then, that our story ends with God twice closing off any further questions from Moses. The first time, Moses modestly wonders why God chose him and not Akiva to receive the original Torah. God tells him to shut up. God takes no questions on the subject. The second time, a horrified Moses questions how Akiva could meet such a gruesome end. God again shuts him up. A story that teaches and glorifies limitless inquiry, infinite interpretive possibilities, ends with God imposing limits.

But the limits are for Moses, a man of the *pshat*, a leader and hero stuck at the surface. God doesn't shut up Akiva. In fact, we know from a different story that Akiva, the hero of *drash*, never gives up searching for, and finding new answers.

> The Sages taught: Four entered the *Pardes* [mystical orchard] and they are as follows, Ben Azzai, Ben Zoma, *Aḥer*, and Rabbi Akiva. Rabbi Akiva said to them: When you reach pure marble stones, do not say "Water, water," because it is stated, "He who speaks falsehood shall not be established before My eyes." (Ps 101:7).
> Ben Azzai glimpsed and died. And with regard to him, the verse states, "Precious in the eyes of the Lord is the death of His pious ones." (Ps 116:15). Ben Zoma glimpsed and was harmed, i.e., he lost his mind. And with regard to him the verse states, "Have you found honey? Eat as much as is sufficient for you, lest you become full from it and vomit it." (Prov 25:16). *Aḥer* chopped down the shoots of saplings. In other words, he became a heretic. Rabbi Akiva came out safely.[3]

2. *Pirke Avot* 5:22.
3. b. Hag. 14b.

How did Akiva "come out safely?" Many commentaries have struggled with this question. The first clue comes from the only bit of dialogue in the story. Akiva warns against saying "Water water," because it might be a "falsehood." Akiva here seems to be cautioning his colleagues not to get stuck in surface conclusions. Just because something looks like water doesn't mean that's what is. Akiva's gift for interpretation, for transcending the *pshat,* saves his life.

But a fuller theology emerges from the deeper question: what is the *Pardes*? Rashi and many others suggest it's mystical or philosophical contemplation, but Eli Wiesel, in his book *Sages and Dreamers*, offers the most interesting, and ultimately the most useful interpretation.[4] He suggests the four friends are contemplating the problem of evil, why an all-powerful benevolent God would allow the innocent to suffer. He points out that each of the three would have lived through the destruction of the second Temple—their Holocaust. They would have personally witnessed the loss of sovereignty, the slaughter of thousands, and the collapse of their theological system. How do we reconcile Israel's defeat, children dying, a city destroyed, with a caring, all-powerful God, who chooses Israel, and whose Presence yearns for Jerusalem? From a *pshat* perspective, you can't.

That stark reality—that God doesn't care or can't intervene—is too much for Ben Azzai and Ben Zoma; one dies, the other goes insane. *Aher,* Elisha Ben Abuyah, embraces the cold theological logic of the disaster and becomes a heretic. Only Akiva survives as a committed Jew because he reads beyond the *pshat.* Using the creative powers of *drash,* he discovers a deeper, hidden truth both in reality and in the text: that there's a world to come, a place where God rewards the righteous fully, and punishes the wicked.[5] The bitter logic of *pshat* destroys Ben Zoma and Ben Azzai, and expels Elisha. *Drash* rescues Akiva, and therefore Judaism.

Another story validates Akiva's theology of reading. Elisha Ben Abuya—Akiva's Pardes companion, known as *Aher,* or "the Other"—sees a young boy follow his father's instructions by climbing a tree, sending away the mother bird, then collecting the eggs. In these actions, the boy fulfills the only two commandments—honoring his parents, and sending away the mother bird— where the Torah explicitly promises a reward of long life. Yet the boy falls from the tree and dies. "Where is his long life?" Elisha

4. Wiesel, *Sages*, 256–70.

5. b. San.101a.

wonders, and abandons Jewish faith. His son-in-law Rabbi Jacob, a follower of Akiva, comments:

> There is not a single precept in the Torah whose reward is [stated] at its side which is not dependent on the resurrection of the dead. [Thus,] in connection with honoring parents it is written, "that thy days may be prolonged, and that it may go well with thee." In reference to the dismissal of the mother bird, it is written, "that it may be well with thee, and that thou mayest prolong thy days." Now, if one's father said to him, "Ascend to the nest, send away the mother bird, and bring me young birds, and he ascends to the nest, dismisses the mother bird, and takes the young, and on his return falls and is killed, where is this child's happiness and where is this child's prolonging of days? But in order that it may be well with thee, means on the day that is wholly good; and in order that thy days may be long, on the day that is wholly long. [that is, heaven].
>
> And Rabbi Joseph adds: "Had *Aher* [Elisha] interpreted this verse as Rabbi Jacob, his daughter's son, he would not have sinned."[6] But Elisha was incapable of understanding the verse like his son-in-law, or like Akiva, because he's stuck in the *pshat*, the literal meaning of the verse, the surface interpretation of what we see and experience in the world. Only a theology that embraces human interpretive creativity can survive the world's harsh reality, and the Torah's seemingly empty promises. Akiva offers a world shimmering with infinite possibilities, just below the surface. Elisha's *pshat* world leaves us with death and tragedy.

———————

Several years ago, my siblings and I were standing in a cemetery on a blustery winter morning in Kansas City, watching our mother's coffin being lowered into her grave. A brain tumor had killed her at age fifty-nine, at a time in her life when she'd overcome several hardships and was finally enjoying herself. Her untimely death screamed out "unfair" to her four children, as it does to countless families who've experienced similar tragedies. As the coffin plopped into the cold ground my sister leaned over to me and said, "That's not her. That's not Mom." My brother, on my other side, whispered, "Of course it's her. Where else would she be?" Later I thought, it's *pshat* versus *drash*. My brother sees the surface reality. My mother's body died, we buried her, and there's no existence beyond the grave, nothing beyond the

6. b. Kid. 39b.

physical world, what we see and experience. My sister imagined another world, an alternate possibility, where my mother's essence was somehow separate from her body. Her corpse was no longer *her*, but *her* still existed, somewhere. "Imagined" is really the only word for it, since she couldn't touch this disembodied world, measure it, or, of course, prove its existence.

Standing between my brother and sister, between *pshat* and *drash*, it occurred to me that I preferred the *drash*. I wanted to look at my mother's grave, now filling up with dirt shoveled in by the mourners, and see something other than the cold earth covering her coffin. At that moment, I *elected* to follow Rabbi Akiva. Not necessarily in his confident discovery of the afterlife in the mysterious words of the Torah, but in his way of reading the text and the world. This was my leap of faith—that there's more to reality than meets the eye, and that I could encounter an infinity of possibilities by studying Torah, which is to say, I could find God in the text, and therefore in the world. Post-modern faith demands these self-conscious leaps of belief. But it's easier for me to believe in God's presence in the text than that God parted the Red Sea, or that Jonah survived being swallowed by a big fish, or that God takes note of and cares about every moment of my life.

If Rabbi Akiva has an antagonist in the Talmud, it's Rabbi Eliezer, particularly in his understanding of the biblical phrase "eye for an eye." Several rabbis, following Rabbi Akiva's system, interpret the words creatively. "God forbid," they say of the *pshat*. The phrase actually means "the monetary value of an eye for an eye." But Rabbi Eliezer, seemingly directing his comment at Akiva, stubbornly insists *mamash*, or "Literally!"[7]

And we can understand why. *Drash* wrenches words out of context and distorts reality. *Pshat* offers at least a surface intellectual integrity.

But *mamash* literally disenchants the world, robbing us of comfort, creativity, and transcendence. It killed Ben Azzai and drove Ben Zoma to madness. It leaves Judaism, along with my mother, buried in the ground, unable to change or grow. I choose *drash*. The crowns in the letters beckon me every time my fingers move across the text. "Turn me and turn me," they whisper. "Everything is here."

———

Philip Graubart is a rabbi and writer living in San Diego, California. He has served congregations in Massachusetts and California. He has also

7. b. B. Kam. 84a.

served in leadership positions at the National Yiddish Book Center, The Shalom Hartman Institute, and the San Diego Jewish Academy, where he now teaches.

There Is No Commander—and Yet, I Am Commanded

—RABBI ARIEL EDERY

MITZVAH OR NO *MITZVAH*? That is the question.

The life of a Jew is all about *mitzvah*—following the commandments. Jewish life begins with a *mitzvah* (circumcision and naming), and ends with a *mitzvah* (burial and mourning observances). And in between those, Jewish life follows *mitzvah* after *mitzvah*: celebrating the holy days, eating Kosher, observing *Shabbat*, giving *tzedakah* (charitable contributions), studying Torah, teaching your children, feeding the hungry, repairing the world, and so many more!

If you read the first sections of this book and noted the notions of God and Torah presented, those embraced and those rejected, you may be asking, "What then, exactly, is a *mitzvah*/commandment?" And you may also be asking, "Why must I do them?" And, for that matter, "Who says I have to?"

Many Jews have clear and simple answers: a *mitzvah* is what God actually said—it is a commandment from the Superior Being. And, since the *mitzvot* are the specific instructions God gave us through our Prophets in Scripture, you'd better listen and do them.

These answers do not work for me. And if you are still reading this book, I suppose they do not work for you either! Sharing the ideas expressed previously in this book, I, too, reject the notion that God is a Big Man, an Omnipotent and Omni-everything Being, a King (or Queen, or ungendered Monarch) who issues orders.

My challenge, our challenge, is to answer the obvious question. If there is no Divine Being issuing commands, then how can we speak of *mitzvah*/commandment? If there is no "Commander," then the concept of a commandment falls through. Is there any way that the concept of *mitzvah* makes sense for a non-theistic Jew like me?

The first impulse is to follow simple logic, i.e., if there is no Commander, there can be no commandments. And yet, as my life as a Jew developed, from my Conservative/Orthodox upbringing and through the next four decades of studying our tradition, I encountered many ideas which give different, and positive, answers to our question. In fact, Jewish tradition is full of ideas and reasons to keep *mitzvot*/commandments, regardless of the Commander!

Some of those answers are presented in philosophical treatises like Maimonides' *Guide for the Perplexed*. Some are presented through poetry and imagery from the Biblical prophets, the Psalms, and medieval Hebrew poetry. Some of them are presented in parables in the Biblical Wisdom books and in classical Rabbinic *midrash*. In this chapter, I cannot comprehensively review all those texts. But I will share some examples of the pearls found in them, ideas that fully embrace and support the validity and the authority of *mitzvah*, without the need for a heavenly Big-Commander-in-Chief to give us marching orders.

TRADITION!

I am a non-theistic Reform Rabbi, and also a deep traditionalist, who can gladly embrace some twelfth-century Jewish thinking on God. According to Maimonides,

> "There exists in the universe a certain force which controls the whole, which sets in motion the chief and principal parts . . . It is the source of the existence of the Universe in all its parts. That force is God. . . It is on account of this force that man is called microcosm, for he likewise possesses a certain principle which governs all the forces of the body, and on account of this comparison God is called 'the Life of the Universe' (Dan 12:7)."[1]

I am also guided by the thousands-year-old Biblical texts, which affirm that God is not a person, and is not a "Big Man," but rather is different from a human essentially, and is more akin to an abstract Force than a Being. The Prophets Amos, Hosea, and Isaiah deny human characteristics to God, and

---

1. Maimonides, *Guide*, 1:72.

often speak of God as a force in nature. The Wisdom literature (especially Ecclesiastes and Proverbs) speaks of God mostly as an impersonal force that is personified in our speech for didactic purposes only.[2]

But let's be clear. Even thinkers with the most abstract notions of God, such as the Prophets, the biblical wisdom writers, and Maimonides, surely lived their lives observing *mitzvot*/commandments. They saw themselves as commanded to live that way, despite their non-theistic notion of God and their non-belief in a Commander who gives orders. Inspired by them, and other great Jewish thinkers, we do not need to imagine a supernatural Being who magically issued commands to have a clear notion of *mitzvah*—of being commanded to behave in certain ways. We may not have a Commander-in-Chief, but we definitely have other sources of divine command.

SOME PEARLS

Look closely at this commandment from the Torah: "*You shall not oppress a stranger, since you yourselves know the feelings of a stranger, for you, too, were strangers in the land of Egypt.*" (Exod 23:9)

While Torah presents this in God's voice, we can see that the source of this *mitzvah* is our own experience. We have experienced oppression, xenophobia, and racism. We have learned how bad these are from experience, and this reminds us to make sure we do not do the same to anyone else.

While some of us experienced Egypt, and some of us experienced the *Shoah*, most Jews in history did not personally live through either of those. In this sense, when we speak of the commandments emerging from our

---

2. While there certainly was in ancient Israel a belief in God as a person with physical and emotional traits, the Prophets often speak differently of God, as the force of nature, God being "*like the dew to Israel, so it blossoms*" (Amos 14:5) and "*rottenness to the House of Judah.*" (Hos 5:12, NRSV) Hosea further emphasizes that we should see no similarity between God and people, "*I am a God, not a person*"(Hos 11:9). Isaiah often insists that God is nothing like a person, not physical but spiritual (Isa 31:3,8), and God's plans and ways are nothing like the humans' thoughts and belong to a different category altogether (Isa 55:8). There are Biblical texts which insist in that God is not אִישׁ—*ish*, a Hebrew word that it is used for man, but also a general term for "person," referring collectively to men, women, children, e.g., "*The Deity is not a person to deceive, nor a human to regret.*" (Num 23:19) The book of Proverbs personifies God, just as it personifies Lady Wisdom, describing God and Wisdom as a loving couple. We certainly understand that wisdom is not a person, but a real and abstract concept personified for didactic effect. As this text speaks of God and Wisdom in the very same terms, this strongly suggests that God is a real, yet abstract, concept personified only for literary purposes.

experience of oppression, we refer both to the personal experiences we may have, and also to the collective and historical experience of generations of Jews. Our personal experience and our historical experience both command us.[3]

Let's look now at what is undoubtedly the most famous commandment in the world, *"You must love your neighbor as yourself."* (Lev 19:18) This commandment is so central in Judaism that the Talmud tells us how Rabbi Hillel used it to summarize the whole of Torah in one phrase, *"What you hate when done to you, do not do it to your fellow—this is the whole Torah!"*[4]

The Golden Rule, which is part of every religion, and is also golden outside of religious communities, is golden precisely because it doesn't matter whether you believe in a God or not. It doesn't matter who is laying down the rule since it includes its own source of authority: empathy. The awareness that others feel pain just like we do is enough for us to see ourselves commanded to not cause that pain to others.

> Another source of commandment comes from the beautiful verses
> of Ps 19:
> "The skies are telling us about a divine wonder;
> A message is expressed day to day,
> knowledge is conveyed night to night;
> But there is no speaking, and there are no words,
> Their voice is not audible."[5]

Indeed, when in deep contemplation of the skies, when exploring and discovering the Universe's grandeur, the skies do speak to us. The universe's beauty, complexity, and power are an eternal source of awe for us. This was true in Biblical times just as it is in our time.

Carl Sagan wrote, "In its encounter with Nature, science invariably elicits a sense of reverence and awe. The very act of understanding is a celebration of joining, merging, even if on a very modest scale, with the magnificence of the Cosmos... Science is not only compatible with spirituality, it is a profound *source* of spirituality. When we recognize our place in

---

3. Judaism can be best understood as the sum of the lessons, sensibilities and behaviors which resulted from our long history on this earth. When he wrote a book with a comprehensive presentation of Judaism, Rabbi Leo Trepp, a *Shoah* survivor, tellingly gave it the title, *"A History of the Jewish Experience."*

4. b. Shab. 31a.

5. Ps 19:1–4, Author's translation.

an immensity of light-years and in the passage of ages, when we grasp the intricacy, beauty, and subtlety of life, then that soaring feeling, that sense of elation and humility combined, is surely spiritual."[6]

Dr. Sagan and the Psalmist share the practice of contemplating, discerning, and marveling at the Universe. They also share the awe that results from that. Yet knowledge of our amazing universe does more than spark awe—it elicits reverence. Reverence is not just a feeling, it includes the call to adjust our behaviors by honoring and respecting the object of our reverence. As Jews, many of the *mitzvot* we follow show precise reverence for life—human life, animal life, the life of the universe, and our natural environment. When I religiously abstain from eating animals as food, and when I act to avoid products and behaviors which degrade the environment (adopting what some call Eco-Kosher), I see myself clearly and directly commanded to do so—by Nature, by Life, by my scientific knowledge, and by my awe of the Universe.

Ps 19, along with the Torah's rules regarding animal suffering, together with many similar Biblical commandments, are not themselves the source that commands me. They are the reminder and the vehicle through which my attention is drawn to the sources that do command me: Nature, Life, Knowledge, Awe, Reverence.[7]

The Talmud teaches explicitly that Torah is simply shorthand, a reminder of the values and behaviors which we ourselves derive through our intellectual and spiritual abilities. As in this text: "Rabbi Yohanan observed, If the Torah had not been given, we could have learned modesty from the cat, honest labor from the ant, marital fidelity from the dove, and good manners from the rooster."[8] Torah does not merely give us mysterious orders. It commands the behaviors that we can learn by carefully observing nature.

The ideas we've been discussing from the Psalms, Biblical Wisdom, Maimonidean philosophy, and Talmudic Rabbis such as Hillel and Yohanan may be condensed in one phrase: We do not do a *mitzvah* because Torah says so, or because it is written that God said so; we do a *mitzvah* because we come to understand that is our responsibility to do so. We do a

6. Sagan, *Demon-Haunted World*, 29.

7. For enlightening discussions on Jewish ethical commands from our tradition regarding animals, all life, and the environment, see *Judaism and Vegetarianism* by Richard H. Schwartz, Lantern Books, New York, 2001, or visit Jewishveg.org.

8. b. Eruv. 100b.

mitzvah because of what we have learned from experience, because of the knowledge we have gained by observing our world, and from studying our history. The Torah's and God's commandments are simply reminders of the expectations and demands that those processes and forces present to us.

Perhaps the best way to conclude is with a suggested definition of *mitzvah*. A *mitzvah* is a responsibility I accept, a behavioral expectation that as a Jew I undertake, and it is one that I fulfill religiously. I do it regardless of my mood or daily schedule. I do it even if it is costly, even if it is inconvenient, even if it is against a personal desire. I prioritize my sense of obligation over my wants and selfish concerns.

On Friday eve, when I fulfill the *mitzvot* of celebrating Shabbat and of communal prayer in my congregation, we read in our prayer book: "As Jews, our main connection with holiness is through acts of *mitzvah*. *Mitzvah* comes from the words of prophets, from Israel's values and traditions; and also from our conscience, from reason, and from what knowledge and wisdom call us to do—for our own good and for the common good. A *mitzvah* is that action we do knowing it is the right thing to do, without needing explanations. We do not perform a *mitzvah* to go up to a holy heaven; we do it to help bring heaven down to our earth. When we engage in a *mitzvah*, we make any time and place become a holy moment and a holy place.[9]

I believe, and have seen time and again, how *mitzvah*—the notion that we are commanded to do something—makes a real difference in people's lives. And I think most Jews (past and present) would agree that the whole point of embracing Judaism's commandments is to have a guide for doing good in this world, a context for doing it, and a community to do it with us. While this ethical drive is at the core of our tradition, many ritual and social practices have been turned into commandments as well. Our Jewish communal context enables us to preserve and continue this religious-ethical life.

Which *mitzvot* should we follow? The list is surely long! On the top of our *Mitzvah* List, I see acting to reduce the oppression and suffering of "the widow, orphan, and the foreigner[10]; working for *Tikkun Olam*—the repair of what is broken in our world; dedication to the pursuit of all knowledge, and using it to shape our lives for better; improving ourselves and our moral character through ethical and ritual practice.

9. Edery, *Siddur*, 46.
10. Exod 22:21–22.

Following the specific practices in Jewish tradition, or even without those traditional forms, I have countless opportunities each day to rise to a *mitzvah*, e.g., in every act I do for society's benefit, in the way I treat others, in the way I treat animals and nature, in the consumption choices I make, in the policies I support or oppose, by engaging in self-improvement and by developing a more virtuous character. I am sure you can add others and create your own *Mitzvah* List, a bar of expectations through which you can grow.

The Prophet Micah said: "God has told you what is good, and what God requires of you: Only to do justice, and to love kindness, and to walk humbly with your God."[11] These are commandments assigned to us by God—which is to say, by Nature, by Reason, by Knowledge, by Conscience, by History, and by Ethics. I trust that we all find these to be powerful Commanders, whose mitzvot we must embrace.

———————

Rabbi Ariel Edery serves congregation Beth Shalom in Raleigh, NC. Born in Argentina into a rabbinic family, he is a graduate of the Hebrew University in Jerusalem and was ordained as a rabbi by the Hebrew Union College. He is also a faculty member at the IIFRR (Reform Rabbinic school for Spain and the Spanish-speaking Americas), where he teaches Bible, Rabbinic Literature, and Midrash.

11. Mic 6:8.

Miracles

—Rabbi Elizabeth Bahar

THE FAMOUS MIRACLE

> A naturalist came from a great distance to see the Ba'al Shem and
> said: "My investigations show that in the course of nature the Red
> Sea had to divide at the very hour the children of Israel passed
> through it. Now, what about that famous miracle?!" The Ba'al Shem
> answered: "Don't you know that God created nature? And he cre-
> ated it so, that at the hour the children of Israel passed through the
> Red Sea, it had to divide. That is the great and famous miracle."[1]

WE SHARE STORIES SO that we can identify with different individuals in
the stories. Whether it is a woman struggling with infertility issues, the
fear in Elijah struggling to find God on a mountain top only to hear the
still small voice responding,[2] or wondering how the world functions as in
the Hasidic story above, these stories help us identify and see the divine
around us. They help us make meaning in our own lives so that we can see
all the events that occur around us as miracles. In the words of Eli Wiesel:
"We must step off the page into our own situation, which is unmapped and
unknown."[3] By knowing the stories on the page, we can step off and start to
create meaning.

---

1. Buber, *Tales*, 71.
2. 1 Kgs 19:12.
3. Burger, *Witness*, 44.

As a Rabbi, I have interacted with people in various life stages: some exciting moments including a *bar/bat mitzvah* or a celebration of a newborn infant. Equally, I have interacted with individuals in painful situations such as the loss of a loved one, job loss, or divorce. In these challenging moments those individuals who were able to see every action that occurred as a blessing/miracle—the good, the bad, and the ugly—were most able to proceed successfully onto the next phase of learning. They were able to place their story into a larger narrative. They identified with either the naturalist or the Ba'al Shem in the Hasidic tale or identified themselves as the Moses of their own life. Alternatively, those who remained in their own pain could only see themselves struggling in the toil of the mud in Egypt waiting to be redeemed. The miracle was when we were able to choose how we crafted our narrative: victim—slave in Egypt or redeemed—Moses the redeemer of self and others.

These stories help us to see ourselves more clearly. When we annually recite these stories from our sacred tradition, we internalize them then we react more deeply to them. We might be able to feel Sarah laughing out loud when she was told she would be pregnant at the young age of one hundred by an angel. "How absurd, that this might come to pass," we can almost hear her saying to herself as she laughs. (Gen 18:12) Then we might see ourselves laughing at some incredible story of a miraculous pregnancy after a fertility doctor said it would be impossible.

We can feel Jacob's anxiety as he leaves his homeland wondering what will happen. He then has a reassuring dream from God that his descendants will have a future (Gen 28:10–19). We might feel like Jacob when faced with a fork in our life, desperate for a sign that we are on the correct path. The dream or sign comes, and we breathe easier knowing that what comes next will be good.

Perhaps we feel symptoms of the imposter syndrome when faced with great challenges as Gideon was in the book of Judges. Gideon required three signs from God, much reassurance before he was able to be successful with a nighttime attack against the Midianites (Judg 7). By identifying with these stories, we can begin to be sensitive to the small daily miracles continuously occurring around us—that God can be present for each individual person simultaneously.

One of the powerful phrases I learned as a student rabbi was a Maya Angelou quote: "I've learned that people will forget what you said, people will forget what you did, but people will never forget how you made them feel."[4] It is not simply human interactions that can cause us to feel and develop sensitivities to the needs of others. We can also develop those same sympathies and increase our empathy with characters in stories and therefore in our own life. Those stories can make us feel triumphant, sad, excited, and anxious.

By not just reading these stories but by studying and excavating them, we can discover additional lessons taught by others who have come along well after the stories were written. Rabbi Solomon Freehof taught the difference between what is a miracle and what is not. He wrote, "Those magicians of Egypt were much like us. When Moses by a miracle turned the Nile to blood, they did so also. When Moses produced another plague, they did so also. So, they were not all impressed. But they soon discovered something disturbing. They could bring the plagues, but they could not remove them."[5] Only by reading for subtleties can we understand the lesson Freehof is offering. Human beings have limitations, God does not. That is what makes Divine interventions miraculous. Human beings can create but may not be able to control.

When we feel lost in our life, unsure of the significance of what we are feeling, we need only turn to our sacred stories for grounding. If we follow the sage advice of Rabbi Ben Bag Bag who said: "Turn it over, and [again] turn it over, for all is therein. And look into it, and become gray and old therein, and do not move away from it, for you have no better portion than it." (*Pirke Avot* 5:22) By continuing to turn and recite, we recognize that we are like all of the characters in our sacred tradition at one point or another. We are able to experience our Torah as something beyond just words on a page, but a narrative that expresses our lives as well.

As we recite these stories, they impact us and sensitize us. The challenge is to go about our day in awe of creation seeing miracles and gifts at every turn.[6] It is easy to walk past a homeless person unaffected. While

---

4. Tunstall, *How Maya Angelou*, para. 2.

5. Freehof, *Spoken and Heard*, 179.

6. "Our goal should be to live life in radical amazement. ....get up in the morning and look at the world in a way that takes nothing for granted. Everything is phenomenal;

reading about "the other," it is harder to walk past a homeless person and have no compassion for them. It is easier to watch someone experiencing strife, believing we are not like them. It is harder to do that while reading stories of Elijah appearing in disguise to help people in distress and to create a sense of peace.[7]

A peculiar phrase in Deut 10:6 shared in the book of Jeremiah suggests to us that the stories make us more sensitive.[8] "Circumcise the foreskin of your hearts–וּמַלְתֶּם אֵת עָרְלַת לְבַבְכֶם." On the face, it makes little sense. How can you circumcise your heart, an internal organ? But we can circumcise our hearts if we open a part of us that was previously closed. The instrument of that circumcision are these stories. In his medieval commentary Rabbeinu Bahya teaches, "You shall 'circumcise' the foreskin surrounding your heart." The term עָרְלָה—orlah is applied when the Torah or the prophet wants to describe a negative character trait, a trait which inhibits development of a personality to its full potential. Anyone who is burdened with such an impediment to his personality development cannot truly embrace the commandments we know as the *mitzvot ha-muskalot*— מצות המושכלות, the deeper meaning of the commandments which are accessible to our intelligence, and to understand their true value.[9]

By allowing ourselves to remove the impediments in our hearts, we can allow deep feelings of awe, compassion, wonder and amazement to fill in. The telling and retelling of our sacred stories helps us remove an impediment around our hearts. It helps us become sensitive to the miracles around us. In the words of Mother Teresa, "In the silence of the heart God speaks. If you face God in prayer and silence, God will speak to you. Then you will know that you are nothing. It is only when you realize your nothingness, your emptiness, that God can fill you with Himself. Souls of prayer are souls of great silence."[10]

It is hard to see miracles around us, or even to believe in them. By reading stories of human struggles, we can contextualize our life in the broader tapestry of the human experience. We can see that suffering

---

everything is incredible; never treat life casually. To be spiritual is to be amazed."—Abraham Joshua Heschel.

7. b. B. Bat. 59b, Shab. 33b, B. Metz. 83b–84a, Sanh. 98a.

8. "To whom shall I speak, Give warning that they may hear? Their ears are blocked And they cannot listen. See, the word of the Lord has become for them an object of scorn; they will have none of it." (Jer 6:10).

9. Rabbenu Bahya, Devarim 10:16:1.

10. Mother Teresa, *In the Heart*, 9.

is temporary, that everything which happens in our life is a miracle and appreciate with awe and amazement the gifts around us. These stories of miracles are not intended to be read literally, rather their fantastical nature allows us to reach a deeper level of understanding and connection of and with the world.

On June 1, 2020, Rabbi Elizabeth Bahar joined the Temple Beth Israel family in Macon Ga. She served the congregation in Jacksonville beginning on July 1, 2018. Prior to that she served as spiritual leader of Temple B'nai Sholom in Huntsville, Alabama for nine years. During her tenure there, she won widespread recognition for promoting the congregation's inclusiveness, innovative programming and welcoming all who entered its doors. The values and traditions she cherishes and her commitment to fostering the closest relationship possible between congregation and clergy are central to her new role at Temple Beth Israel.

Rabbi Bahar was ordained in 2009 by Hebrew Union College–Jewish Institute of Religion, where she also earned her Master of Arts in Hebrew Letters. Before that, she was a rabbinic intern at Adath Israel Congregation in Cincinnati, a student rabbi at Anshe Emeth in Pine Bluff, Arkansas, and Temple Shalom in Winnipeg, Canada. She also earned a BA in philosophy at Brandeis University. Rabbi Bahar is president of the South East Central Conference of American Rabbis. She was recognized by The Forward as one of "America's 33 Most Inspirational Rabbis" in 2015.

Rabbi Bahar is the proud parent of a daughter, Aiden, and two sons, David and Daniel.

Hebrew Lessons

To Discover the Divine,
To Reveal the Truly Human

—Rabbi Mark Joel Mahler

What time is it? Hint: Don't bother to look at a clock.

Shamayim--שמים is Hebrew for Heaven. Etymologically, *Shamayim* derives from the Akkadian word for Heaven—*Shamu*. But casting a rabbinic eye upon *Shamayim* as Heaven appears in Hebrew throughout the Bible, we see two Hebrew words, *sham*—שם, there and *mayim*—מים, water emerge therein. Because the Hebrew infinitive, *L'hiyot*—להיות, to be, has no present tense verbs, Hebrew has no equivalents to is, am, or are in English. Rather, Hebrew subsumes these verbs in context. Therefore, *Shamayim*, translates into English, There is Water.

No surprise that our ancestors should associate Heaven with water. Our ancestors were semi-nomadic shepherds, then farmers, whose existence depended on meager sources of water in the arid Levant. There, rain falls but one-half of the year while sun scorches the land the other half. Yet our ancestors saw something far deeper than just water in the wells and springs, the seasonal rains and wadis that sustained them. They saw Heaven, *Shamayim*—There is Water. Our ancestors' profound insight equating water to Heaven compels us to ask, where is water?

Had our planet been properly named, it would be Water, not Earth. Water covers three-quarters of our planet's surface. The iconic photograph of the Blue Marble taken by astronauts en route to the moon captures the beauty of water's preponderance. Massive oceans contain ninety-six percent of our Blue Marble's water. Downy swirls of water-laden clouds bedeck

116

our Blue Marble. Lakes and ponds dot the land. Rivers and brooks meander about. These waters transform barren sand and hard clay into verdant soil. Beneath their surface, all waters teem with life. In these waters, sentient life emerged eons ago. From these waters, our species evolved.

We human beings are water, sixty-percent water overall, from the hair crowning our head to the nails protecting our toes, to the bones that keep us upright and mobile. Water especially saturates our organs. Every cell of our heart and brain is three-quarters water. Blood, *Dam*--דם in Hebrew, the site of the soul according to the Torah, is ninety-percent water. And lest a mixture of oxygen plus nitrogen alone damage the delicate alveoli of our lungs, water vapor permeates the air we breathe.

What would we do without water? Without food we can live for weeks. Without water we will perish in a matter of days.

So, where is water?

Water surrounds us. Water suffuses us. To borrow from Samuel Coleridge's *The Rime of the Ancient Mariner*, Water, water is everywhere, within us and all around us!

So where then is heaven?

The word *Shamayim* teaches that Heaven, like water, surrounds us. Heaven, like water, suffuses us. Heaven is everywhere, within us and all around us. *Shamayim* reveals a new, higher and deeper rhyme:

Heaven, heaven, everywhere,
So all should stop and think,
How Heaven, Heaven, everywhere
Our heart and soul do drink.
In simple terms, we are in Heaven.

Having found Heaven in physical terms, our search returns us to our first question. What time is it?

It is Now.

When asked previously, it was now then, but then is no longer now. It is now now . . . and now . . . and now. . . It is always now.

Now may be the most obvious aspect of our existence, yet we overlook it so often that it deserves to be capitalized: Now! Now is the only moment in time that we ever truly experience because it is always Now.

As *Shamayim* teaches that we are in heaven "physically," Now teaches that we are in Heaven "temporally." Note "quotes," because *Shamayim* and Now awaken us to expand our previous understandings of existence's physical and temporal dimensions. Heaven is in us Now, flowing from head to toe, through heart and soul. We are in Heaven Now, all around us to the outermost fringes of the universe. All beings—physical, temporal, earthly, and heavenly—merge in the eternal Now as one.

Only one thing exceeds all this: the God who created all this, the God who Judaism proclaims as One.

God has many Hebrew names, but *YHWH* is the superlative. *YHWH* derives from the aforementioned infinitive, *L'hiyot*—To Be. *YHWH* may be the closest Hebrew equivalent to a present tense form of is, am, or are. But *YHWH* is not a verb. Rather, it serves as a proper noun. What might this name, The Name, mean in English?

Consider when Moses asked God's name as they met at the Burning Bush. God answered, *Ehyeh-Asher-Ehyeh*—אהיה אשר אהיה, translated roughly into English as, "I am that I am," or "I will be what I will be." How exquisitely *ad infinitum* applies here! It is simply *Ehyeh*. The Jewish Publication Society's translation committee, comprised of twentieth-century America's greatest biblical scholars and Hebraists, chose not to translate God's answer into English, opting solely for the English transliteration, as above. Of note, nowhere else in Torah is God known by these appellations, whereas their sacred shorthand, *YHWH*, occurs thousands of times, far more than any of God's other Hebrew names.

The traditional Hebrew euphemism for *YHWH* is *Adonai*, because the ineffable Name is unpronounced. The traditional English translation of *Adonai* as Lord smacks of anthropomorphism and obscures God's supreme divinity. A contemporary rendering, The Eternal, may approach an English meaning of *YHWH*. Yet while capturing God's transcendence, The Eternal lacks God's quintessential immanence. Our medieval rabbis coined the euphemism, *HaMakom*—המקום, The Place, for God, expressing God's immanence as The Place for all existence, but lacking God's equally quintessential transcendence.

What hews closest to *YHWH*'s meaning in English when pared down to its essence derived from *L'hiyot*—To Be, is Is-ness. Is-ness! All that is, is in God. And all Is-ness is eternally Now.

Millenia before Shakespeare asked rhetorically, "What's in a name?," Judaism knew: Everything! Holding true for every name, this is surpassingly true for *YHWH*. Various passages throughout the Bible describe God as loving, compassionate, merciful, just, impassioned, forgiving, gracious, mighty, exalted, holy, faithful, long suffering, first and last, eternal, immanent and transcendent, etc. Simultaneously, first and foremost, and stretching the human mind beyond comprehension, God is One. In God's name *YHWH*—Is-ness, all this is captured, and more.

———————

What then are the past and the future?

They too are God's creation. "Was-were" and "Will be" have their place and purpose in the eternal realm of Is-ness.

Memory enshrines the past. Memory acculturates us to social norms, putting civility in civilization. Because memory is learning's *sine qua non*, Judaism is grounded in memory, from *B'reshit*—בראשית, The Beginning of existence, until Now. Many species in the animal kingdom exhibit the ability to learn and remember, but *homo sapiens'* superior ability to learn and remember, think, and teach has placed us at the pinnacle of evolution. Rabbi Akiva described our evolutionary preeminence, "Beloved is man that he was created in the image of God, but it is by force of a special love that it was made known to us that he was created in the image of God."[1]

On the personal level, memory serves a uniquely tender role. Memory preserves in the present our loved ones who have passed. Memory revivifies them, blurring and blending distinctions between life and death, the eternal Now and eternal life. Dreams of loved ones who have passed are but one portal to these transcendent insights and experiences. To dream such dreams taps dreams' potency, a theme Torah powerfully underscores.[2]

Memory and death intertwining also take us to deeper dimensions of heart and soul. Memory can overwhelm us with grief. Memory can also comfort us with warmth and sweetness. Ultimately we must ask, which is more loving? To forget our loved ones and rid ourselves of pain, or to remember our loved ones and accept the pangs of love eternal? The service of *Yizkor Neshamot* assures us that as we remember our loved ones' souls, God remembers them as well. When we walk through these valleys of the

1. *Pirke Avot* 3:14.

2. Dreams are central to the Book of Genesis in particular, viz. Jacob in chapter 28, Joseph in chapter 37, the butler and baker in chapter 40, Pharaoh in chapter 41, and again Jacob in chapter 46.

shadow of death let us fear no evil, for God is with us; God's rod and staff comfort us.[3] These are among the precious gems in the treasure chest of memory.

While Judaism is grounded in the past, Judaism ever impels us toward the future. The future's glorious promise existed from The Beginning, but hidden. The promise was repeated, writ larger at the Burning Bush, but still hidden. All that was needed to perceive the glorious promise was imagination.

If not for imagination, how could God create the universe *ex nihilo*—from nothing, no less? How could sentient life evolve on this planet, no doubt on innumerable planets throughout myriad galaxies across this vast universe? Existence bears witness to God's imagination.

Dimyon—דמיון is Hebrew for imagination. Casting a rabbinic eye again, within *Dimyon* we see *Dam*—Blood, noted above as the site of the soul in Torah. Blood animates the life of every species in the animal kingdom, but *Dimyon*, imagination, is a gift God shared with us superabundantly, among the rare attributes whereby God created us in the Divine image. Like another divine gift, Free Will, when placed in human hands, imagination can be for good or for evil. Using Now for good, God's sole intention, we reveal what otherwise seemed hidden.

The *Shoresh*, or root, of the Torah's first word, *B'reshit*, are the Hebrew letters *Resh*, *Aleph* and *Shin*, spelling *Rosh*—ראש, Head. The traditional translation of *B'reshit*, "In the beginning," is a reasonable rendering, but it misses the utter verity of the more literal translation, "In the head," i.e., "In God's head," or if you will, "In God's imagination." The Kabbalistic practice of *Tzeruf* permutates the letters of a Hebrew root to yield a new meaning with even deeper verity to the root. In this case, *Resh*, *Aleph* and *Shin*, spelling *Rosh*—Head, permutate into *Aleph*, *Shin*, *Resh*, which spells *Osher*—אשר, Happiness. Happiness was in God's Head from The Beginning.

The selfsame Hebrew letters are also in the middle of God's Name disclosed at the Burning Bush, *Ehyeh Asher Ehyeh*. In this context, *Asher* is commonly translated as That or What. However, since the Torah lacks vowels, *Asher* can be vocalized again as *Osher*—Happiness! Thus, God's Name is I am Happiness, I am, or I will be Happiness, I will be!

In this reading, from the Beginning, God promised the happily ever after future, reaffirmed to Moses at the Burning Bush to redeem a people suffering slavery, the ultimate human indignity.

---

3. Adapted from Ps 23:4.

It sounds simple. It has proven otherwise.

In a consummate expression of love for us created in God's image, God also blessed us with free will. So Adam and Eve exercised their free will, defying God's request, and ate the forbidden fruit. The rest is history.

In antiquity, our patriarchs and prophets responded to God's call with the singular Hebrew word for being present in the Now: *Hineni*—הנני, Here I am![4] They tried to steady humankind's wayward, willful course by envisioning the idyllic future when "nation shall not lift up sword against nation; they shall never again know war."[5] These words reverberate across the centuries, too often unheeded. If only all humanity could realize all that is present Now.

Hebrew has two words for Now: *Ahshav*—עכשיו and *Ata*—עתה. *Ahshav*, the modern term, is nowhere to be found in the Bible. *Ata*, the biblical term, is revelatory. *Ata* is a homophone, a rarity in Hebrew. When homophones do occur in Hebrew, they brim with significance. *Ata*, beginning with the letter *Ayin*, is Now. *Ata*—אתה, beginning with the letter *Aleph*, is You. *Ani* is another Hebrew homophone. Beginning with *Aleph*, *Ani*—אני is I. Beginning with *Ayin*, *Ani*—עני is Poor.

As Hillel would say, *Zil G'mor*—Come and Learn[6] what these Hebrew homophones, *Ani* and *Ata*, teach. I am Poor. You are Now. Please repeat these until they permeate your consciousness.

If we seek to understand the depth and breadth of being created in God's image we must rid ourselves of the self-involvement, the narcissism, and the solipsism that debase our higher human nature. Who we are is fully realized only in relation to the other, to the you before us, moment by eternal moment, and ultimately to the You before all, the Is-ness of All, *YHWH*, God.

4. Abraham in Gen 22:1, Jacob in Gen 27:1, Moses in Exod 3:4, Samuel in 1 Sam 3:4, Isa 6:8.

5. Isa 2:4; Mic 4:3.

6. b. Shab. 31a.

In the Torah's most rapturous moment between God and man, God says to Moses, "You cannot see My face, for man shall not see Me and live."[7] Yet, Moses' epitaph in the Torah clearly states that Moses knew God face to face.[8] Elsewhere in Torah, God's face is palpable, as in *Birkat Kohanim*—the Priestly Blessing, not merely once but twice: "May God's face shine upon you. . ." and "May God lift up His face to you. . ."[9] And it is intended not merely for one select individual but for the entire people.

The most enlightening moment about the revelation of God's face follows Jacob's famous wrestling match. "Jacob called the name of the place *Pene-El*—פניאל, the Face of God—'for I have seen God face to face and my life has been spared.'"[10] The next day, Jacob and Esau have their tearful reconciliation after twenty years of bitter estrangement. Responding to the many gifts that Jacob had lavished upon him, Esau says, "I have much of my own, brother, let that which is yours be yours."[11] But Jacob graciously insists that Esau accept his gifts, saying, ". . . because seeing your face is like seeing the face of God."[12]

In the annals of Jewish experience, who knew better than Jacob the "face of God?" Just the night before, Jacob had encountered God so palpably that he named that place Face of God. The very next day, Jacob tells his brother that seeing his face is like seeing the face of God!

But wait! There is no Hebrew word Face. The Hebrew word *Panim*—פנים literally means Faces. How true. Our forty-three facial muscles interact to give each one of us thousands of faces. And God's faces? God currently has 7.7 billion potential faces here on earth, beings uniquely created in God's image.

When we do what God asks of us, God then lives in us and we become a face of God. For the Jewish people, whenever we keep a *mitzvah* we become a face of God. Any and every human being becomes a face of God when they "do justly, love mercy, and walk humbly with God."[13]

---

7. Exod 33:20.
8. Deut 34:10.
9. Num 6:25–26.
10. Gen 32:31.
11. Gen 33:9.
12. Gen 33:10.
13. Mic 6:8.

Imagine living in a world where everyone you see is one of God's innumerable faces. Imagine living in a world where everyone sees you as one of God's innumerable faces. Therein lies the promise of the future.

The Torah describes God as Most-Mighty, never Almighty, starting with the forbidden fruit. Truer still is this description of God today, in our Age of I-dolatry, the deification of the self and the casual disregard, even callous contempt, for the Other, be they animal, vegetable or mineral.

How close can the promise of the future be fulfilled in *Ata*, in Now—עתה and You—אתה? Yet how distant it remains.

In the meantime, God's sacred energy holds everything together: Love. This English word derives from the Hebrew *Lev*—לב, Heart. In Hebrew, Love is *Ah-Ha-Va*—אהבה. Said as written, syllable by syllable, it is the sound of breathing. Every heartbeat, every inhale, every exhale energizes existence, from every cell in our body to the farthermost star in the universe, with love, in love, and because of love, here and in Heaven, Now and eternally.

Rabbi Mark Joel Mahler was ordained at Hebrew Union College-Jewish Institute of Religion in New York in 1978. He is now rabbi emeritus at Temple Emanuel of South Hills, Pittsburgh, where he served from 1980 until his retirement in 2018.

PART III

BELIEVABLE HOLINESS

God Knows What Path We Are On

—Rabbi Anson Laytner

I. WHAT KIND OF GOD?

The Jewish perception of God has always been rooted in experience. Whether starting with Moses' experience of God's presence in the burning bush or with the people of Israel's experience of God at Mt. Sinai,[1] those seminal, mythic experiences of the divine were sufficient to fuel the Jewish faith for over three millennia—and indeed to propel the development of both Christianity and Islam as well. But no longer.

Today, experience has led many Jews in a different direction.

First and foremost, the *Shoah* (Holocaust), which was the culmination of centuries of persecution in Christian Europe, has led many Jews to doubt the assumption, if not the existence, of a supernatural God who intervenes in the lives both of individuals and whole nations. This experience of unprecedented Jewish suffering in the *Shoah* is a counterpoint to the story of our ancestors' experience of the God they perceived acting on behalf of Israel during the exodus from Egypt. This has provoked a number of responses.

Many people accused God of ignoring the suffering and death of so many millions of people. If God could have acted but chose not to, then this raises serious doubts about God's love and compassion for the Jews. Other people claimed to see God as actively involved in the *Shoah* but only

---

1. See, for example, how Yehudah HaLevi develops Judaism as an experience-based faith in his book *Sefer HaKuzari*—The Book of the Kuzari, in which he argues that 600,000 eyewitnesses at Sinai cannot be wrong.

acting to save specific individuals and groups on a small scale. This claim, however, ignores the scope of the catastrophe and makes for a capricious God. If God could save a few, why not the many; and why these and not those? Still others saw God as using the Nazis and their allies to punish the Jewish people for some alleged sin, be it killing Christ, assimilating to European norms, creating Reform Judaism, or embracing Zionism. Although this claim remains true to the Biblical/Rabbinic theology of suffering-is-punishment-for-sins-committed, given the scope of the death and destruction, it turns God into an abusive monster. Some assert that the *Shoah* had everything to do with human behavior, that God has given humans the gift of free will and therefore we need to deal with the consequences of humans' choices. Yet others would aver that there is no God to worry our heads about. But both of these last two views stand the traditional Jewish understanding of God's role in human history on its head.

The second component to our changing perception of God is the secularizing forces of modern science, history, and archeology, which have undermined the cosmology, history, and theology of Jewish tradition. Our perception of the universe is neither that of the *Tanakh* (Hebrew Bible) nor of the ancient Rabbis. Consequently, our theology cannot be theirs, either. (Since we can send rockets to Mars and far beyond, where exactly is the "abode of God" for us?) Our age needs to craft a perception of God that fits with our increasingly secularized worldview.

The third component is the perennial experience of personal suffering. In every generation, most people experience personal losses and tragedies in one form or another. This is part of living and it always has been. Reconciling experiences such as these with an omnipotent and loving God has never been an easy task (see the Book of Job) and it is even harder in our own day.

So, whether God is perceived as inactive, active in minor ways, or actively abusive, these perceptions negate the understanding of God's benevolent role in human life as depicted in Torah and reinforced in the *siddur, haggadah,* and *mahzor*—the mainstays of traditional popular Jewish theology.

II. THE ROLE OF THE RABBI

Polls show, and this is backed up empirically, that synagogue attendance is not what it used to be.[23] People have voted with their feet and the kind of Jewish theology that sustained our people for the last two thousand years no longer suffices. This has serious implications for the rabbinic profession. Many rabbis today see themselves as custodians of tradition, doing their best to preserve, present and interest their congregants in a carefully curated collection of artifacts from the Jewish past. While this certainly is a worthwhile task, and it definitely corresponds to what many congregations also seek from their rabbis, a rabbi should also strive to serve as a spiritual teacher, or as I prefer to say, a physician of the Jewish soul.

To fulfill this role will not be easy; but it is urgently needed because our people's connection to our ancestral faith and culture—its pulse—is weakening.

The phenomenon of trans-generational trauma as a secondary form of PTSD has been well-studied across various cultures. But I believe that the spiritual trauma of the *Shoah* has been left largely unaddressed by many congregational rabbis and Jewish theologians because the conflict between the interventionist God of Sinai and the inactive God of Auschwitz is too great to be easily resolved. Add to this individual encounters with tragedy, disease, and death and you have a real crisis of faith among large portions of our people. And, since there is no Jewish place currently to discuss this, the untreated trauma has resulted in an imperfect healing of the modern Jewish soul. The function of the rabbi as physician of the Jewish soul is to remove the superficial spiritual scar tissue that has formed, reopen the theological wound in a controlled way, and allow the wound to heal from the deep inside out. As physicians of the Jewish soul, the rabbi's primary task is to unsettle Jewish minds and hearts. This is how spiritual scar tissue is removed and true healing begins. It will make some Jews angry and it

---

2. Pew Research Center, "Belief in God," Chart 2. In which only 64% of Jews surveyed believe in God compared with the general population's 83%. The Center's 2013 Portrait of American Jews,

3. Pew Research Center, "Jewish American Beliefs," para. 5. Which showed that 62% of those surveyed view being Jewish as an ancestry or culture and 68% said that one doesn't need to believe in God to be a Jew. 22% identified themselves as having no religion, a number close to that of the general population (20%). Among millennials, the percentage was 32%.

will make other Jews uncomfortable but it will make many Jews breathe a sigh of relief.

However, *this cannot take place during a worship service; it must take the place of the worship service.* If people gather once a week, or once a month, or even once a year, then we rabbis must do our best to challenge them spiritually when they are present, so that their Jewish souls are stirred up before they leave.

Healing will begin to happen only when Jews have a serious and sustained conversation, group therapy if you will, about the *Shoah* and their personal tragedies, and the ramifications of these experiences for our God-concepts, the purpose of prayer, and the meaning of being Jewish. And once the flame is rekindled, perhaps much that we Jews worry about will diminish in scope. Perhaps even alienated Jews will return to participate in the discussion.

Sadly, the topic of spirituality, including God-talk, is all but taboo in many congregations. So, it will be up to the rabbi and congregational lay leaders to engender a culture that sustains a safe place for such a conversation and enhances the opportunity for spiritual exploration.

III. THE NEW SYNAGOGUE

Despite what I've written above, I know this ain't going to happen without a significant change in focus. Synagogues will remain primarily places of occasional worship. Learning will focus on providing children with the rudiments of Jewish culture to enable them to reach *Bar/Bat Mitzvah*. Rabbis will continue to serve primarily as quasi-priests: leading worship services, giving sermons, offering pastoral counseling, and conducting life cycle rituals. It is therefore important to focus on the real rather than the ideal.

Given that Jewish culture today, everywhere except in Israel, is built around the synagogue as a house of prayer, our initial focus needs to be on transforming the worship experience.

The Jewish liturgy is comprised of prayers of praise, petition, penitence, and thanksgiving, which, in addition to their obvious intent, are mostly either direct or backhanded ways of teaching our people what to believe and how to conduct themselves. How would this change?

First, we can offer a liturgy that honors contemporary experience of the divine. This is counterintuitive. Most people do not experience the divine in a synagogue but this is what we ask of people when we gather to worship. So how do we create an environment that is conducive to spiritu-ality? Music is of great help in promoting a sense of the spiritual as is time for personal reflection that, I duly note, may be stimulated by the liturgy itself. But we also ought to include time when we gather for people to share how they've experienced God, both in their good times and their bad. In doing this, we would thereby honor the present as well as the past because God has been experienced by many individuals down through the ages, right up to and including the present.

Second, given the challenges presented by the *Shoah*, we could add prayers of protest to our worship. Jewish tradition offers a treasure trove of such prayers, which call God to account for perceived injustice and ap-parent apathy to suffering.[4] Adding in some of these prayers of protest as well as our own protests would inject a note of reality into a traditional worship experience. Personally, I still find value in prayers of praise and thanksgiving, especially for Creation and life's blessings. But I no longer offer petitionary prayers because if God can ignore the *Shoah*, then why ask God to pay attention to our minor requests? If one still believes in an interventionist God, then prayers of protest, which are appeals for atten-tion, justice, and action, are the only petitionary prayers worth making in our post-*Shoah* era.

Third, as we develop new and different conceptions of God, we can begin to formulate a new *siddur*. I see us writing new prayers, revising others, and rejecting others. Undoubtedly, we would want to leave some intact for historical and theological reasons, with notes explaining their context and meaning. This would connect our generation with the prayers of previous generations, establishing us as the latest link in a chain of Jew-ish worship that began with sacrifices, was transformed as prayer by the rabbis in ancient times, and was re-envisioned again by the Jewish mystics and yet again by the early Reformers. Writing a new *siddur* would be a major undertaking, particularly if we consider revising the Hebrew and not just being creative with the English. There is also the question of the Torah service. Would we continue to read from it as we do now for the sake of historical continuity or would we read it with disclaimers, the way we wish Christians would when they read the anti-Jewish portions of the Gospels? Would we go so far as to remove the Torah from the sanctuary and place

4. See Anson Laytner, *Arguing with God: A Jewish Tradition,* (Northvale, NJ: Jason Aronson, 1990) and David Blumenthal, *Facing the Abusing God: A Theology of Protest,* (Louisville: Westminster/John Knox Press, 1993).

it, reverentially but unread, in the library? How far do we go for the sake of consistency?

Fourth, although I believe we need to create a revised *siddur,* how do we arrive at a shared vision of the divine that in any way approximates the breadth and depth of the traditional God? I have to wonder to whom (or what) our prayers would be addressed. To *Adonai* (Lord)? To *Shekhinah* (the divine feminine presence)? To *En Sof* (the Infinite), *Mekor Hayyim* (Source of Life) or something else again? The Hebrew verb "to pray" is reflexive and its meanings include "to judge," so perhaps our prayers are best addressed to ourselves? Perhaps silent meditation is an option, but group silence makes many people, including Jews, anxious. Since we rabbis are trained in a traditional manner, it might be hard for us to imagine what the alternatives to traditional prayer might be. It would be like asking a Temple priest to imagine worshiping God without sacrifices. Perhaps we don't need prayer at all, even in a reimagined form, although there is great value in gathering together and bonding as a community over our shared heritage and common values.

However, if we want to maintain some connection with the anthropomorphic God of Jewish tradition, then at least we ought to address God with a given name. "God" is not a name, it's a job description and, as the Yiddish poet Jacob Glatstein once lamented, God is universal, not particular, and he urged both God and the Jewish people to begin again as smaller entities.[5] The other Abrahamic faiths call God by their own unique names: Christians have Jesus and Muslims have Allah. It's time we start calling on God with God's Jewish name: *Yah. Yah,* which is short for YHVH (the traditionally ineffable divine name), is commonly found in words such as "*halleluYah.*" *Yah,* as opposed to God, is uniquely Jewish and is a name that resonates with historical meaning. *Yah,* unlike God, has no immediate negative baggage associated with it. *Yah,* standing in for YHVH, is the essence of the divine because YHVH is a name constructed from the past, present, and future tenses of the verb "to be." *Yah* connotes Be-ing, past, present, and future. *Yah* is the perpetual flow of living potential and the Source of Life itself, the One who was perceived by Avraham, Moshe, Yisrael at Sinai, and our people down through the ages.[6]

5. See "The Beginning" in *Jacob Glatstein Poems,* translated by Etta Blum, (Tel Aviv: I. L. Peretz Publishing, 1970, 52–56.

6. Yehudah HaLevi in *Sefer HaKuzari* differentiates between *Elohim,* as the God perceived by the intellect, and *Adonai,* standing in for *YHVH,* the God apprehensible through revelation and the prophetic experience. *YHVH* corresponds to God's purported

My point about the *siddur* and prayer is this. After the destruction of the Second Temple, the Rabbis were forced to recreate Jewish worship without the sacrificial cult. They turned to the proto-synagogue worship that coexisted with the Temple and began to radically transform Jewish theology and prayer until we ended up with the *siddur* and worship as we know it today. I like to think our age is on a spiritual cusp not unlike that of the early centuries of the Common Era when our people switched from sacrifices to prayers. Today, I believe, we are gradually switching from prayers directed to an anthropomorphic and supernatural sovereign God to a new synthesis: an experience and naming of the divine that can resonate with our past but also with the world we live in now.[7]

At this point, I would like to return to what I hinted at earlier: a change of direction from the synagogue as primarily a place of prayer (*Bet Tefilah*) to the synagogue primarily as a place of assembly (*Bet Knesset*), which is the original meaning of Synagogue. It could be a place where Jews come to learn and discuss together, to experiment and invent, to collaborate and coalesce. This would entail a shift in focus by both the congregation and the rabbi. Worship and life-cycle rituals could be primarily lay-led, leaving the rabbi freer to focus on teaching and offering guidance. By de-emphasizing worship in favor of study, our people would have time and opportunity both to learn from Jewish sources and to do the kind of talk therapy that is necessary to process trauma like the *Shoah*—and the many other traumas throughout Jewish history. Instead of attempting to revise the *siddur* prematurely, let's focus on reshaping the home rituals that people observe on *Shabbat* and on festivals, and on the values by which we live our daily lives. Let's try to build into Jewish home practice modern theological ideas and prayers that are consistent with them. Instead of theology, we could focus on key Jewish values that transcend all our diverse views of the divine and the *mitzvot*. Over time, and using the synagogue more as a place

---

self-description to Moshe as *Ehyeh* and *Ehyeh-Asher-Ehyeh* in *Shemot*/Exod 3:14.

7. As we begin this process, we should evaluate the innovations currently being done in Aleph-aligned congregations, in the Jewish Emergent Network, by the *Kohenet* Hebrew Priestess Institute, *Chabad,* and other groups. We also might do well to look at how various non-Jewish theologians, e.g., Marcus Borg, Shelby Spong, Thomas Keating, David Steindl-Rast, and others deal with these issues. Or how Jewish thinkers like Jordan Paper and Jay Michaelson bring Chinese and Buddhist perspectives to bear on contemporary Jewish thought.

for learning and discussion, we will have a much better foundation upon which to build a renewed Jewish faith.[8]

I will conclude with a parable of sorts. There was a time when the *halakha* was forgotten by the rabbis in a certain area and they did not know the tradition on how a person could carry a sacrificial knife on *Shabbat* eve to the Temple in Jerusalem. A rabbi from a foreign land, although he too could not remember the rule, exclaimed, "Leave it to Israel. If they are not prophets, then they are the descendants of prophets." And on the next day, the rabbis observed that the person bringing a lamb to sacrifice stuck the knife in its wool and the person bringing a goat wedged the knife between its horns. The people provided the Rabbis with the answer.[9]

In fact, the Rabbis of the Talmud had a rule based on this: "go out and see what the people are doing—*puk hazi mai ama davar.*" Normally, the rabbis tried to argue the law through rigorous reasoning. But in fourteen places in the Talmud they determined the law by going out into the community and seeing what the Jewish people were doing.[10] The implication of this principle is that the wisdom of the people sometimes supersedes that of the sages. The Rabbis generally set the communal standards but occasionally the people did the leading. If the people did not follow the Rabbis by accepting their edicts, those laws would have fallen by the wayside. What we consider Judaism today is only what the people took upon themselves to observe. What the people said at Sinai remains as relevant today as it was back then: "*Na'aseh v'nishma*—we will do and (then) we will listen."[11]

The moral of the story is this: rabbis should not rush to build a post-*Shoah* Judaism based solely on their own thinking. Be patient. Listen to the people and observe what they do. Lead by following. The rest is commentary.

———————

8. I sometimes look at the Jewish people as I imagine an amoeba moves through its life. One edge of the amoeba will move in one direction and the rest of the organism will follow. Then it can change direction and the organism will flow in that direction. Similarly, as a living entity, the Jewish people may explore a reform and flow in that direction for a while, then it may move in a more traditional direction for a time. Any direction is possible—and sometimes multiple directions may compete simultaneously. It all depends on whether or not the body follows a particular leading edge as it pursues its best path to survival.

9. Based on b. Pes. 66a.

10. See, for example, b. Eruv. 14b.

11. Exod 24:7.

Anson Laytner is a retired rabbi, living in Seattle, whose career in non-profit and academic settings focused on fostering positive interfaith and interethnic relations. He is the current president of the Sino-Judaic Institute and editor of its journal *Points East*. He is past president of Northwest Interfaith and has long been active in local interfaith affairs. A graduate of York University (Toronto), Hebrew Union College (Cincinnati), and Seattle University, Laytner is the author of *Arguing with God* (1990), co-author of *The Animals' Lawsuit Against Humanity* (2005), co-editor of *The Chinese Jews of Kaifeng* (2017), and author of *The Mystery of Suffering and the Meaning of God* (2019). Rabbi Laytner is married to Richelle Harrell. He has two living daughters, three sons-in-law, and five grandkids. Contact him via his website: www.ansonlaytner.com.

Life Cycles and Brain Cycles
Finding God in the Body's Journey Through Time

—Rabbi Rami Schwartzer

"A POEM BEGINS AS *a lump in the throat, a sense of wrong, a homesickness, a lovesickness. It finds the thought and the thought finds the words.*"—Robert Frost

Mirroring other inductive learning processes we undergo in our lives, it is helpful to first experience what God feels like in the brain and body before turning to the religious language that allegedly describes Divine encounters. In this order, Torah may take on new meaning that can offer us pathways to living lives of deeper fulfillment and contentment. By starting in the body, we can open the gates of access to God and religious language without first requiring abstract philosophical understanding. I believe this is the way religion and religious language developed originally, and that it is a helpful exercise for contextualizing and connecting with religious concepts in our own contemporary context.

I was first inspired to write theology by my beloved teacher Neil Gillman, of blessed memory, who imparted two heart-opening lessons to me. One was that he stopped believing many of the ideas he published in his seminal book on theology, which he corrected orally before assigning passages for his students to read. The second was that if he were to go back and redo college in his old age, he would have studied neuroscience instead of philosophy, since we cannot ask questions about knowledge until we first understand how it is our brains even formulate ideas.

Gillman's first insight taught me that theology is dynamic, just as we are; his second taught me that God can be understood through observable frameworks that are built into nature. If epistemology presupposes an understanding of the brain, then theology presupposes an understanding of one's own body. Faith follows, rather than precedes, experience. I don't *believe in* God, as if God is an entity whose existence can be refuted. I *experience* God, and I read religious texts with the hope of articulating or clarifying the memory of that experience. We can (and must) use our bodies to access the disembodied concept of God. After all, the only way to leave a house is through an exit intentionally carved into the architecture of the building.

So what is that experience of the body that spawned robust religious traditions of prophecy, revealed wisdom, and an intricate system of behavioral norms? Certainly it is idiosyncratic, as is anything related to the body. But it is also a universal experience of the human nervous system that is accessible to all of us if only we attune our senses to be aware of it when it arrives. My own experiences of God fit into what Julie Holland would call triggering the parasympathetic nervous system.[1] This somatic experience is a mindset of clarity and calm, the grounded confidence I feel when I can think straight and perceive my environment with precision rather than a presupposition. In this state of mind, I become aware of the acute subconscious functions of my body's systems as they operate. It feels as though my consciousness aligns with the numerous natural processes of my body and surrounding environment, of being "at one" with nature. It is no irony that Judaism's first theological innovation was the certainty that God is One—not that there is one God instead of many, but that the word God is synonymous with a feeling of unity.[2]

Because of the stresses of modern life, many of us spend more time in fight-or-flight mode than we do in parasympathetic mode, and may even lack the language or awareness to distinguish between these two states of mind. Our cultural emphases largely fail to cultivate this kind of awareness in the developing minds of children, at least before pressure and anxiety build a nest in their consciousness, making it harder to conjure up this state of mind as they grow. Consequently, the first time someone becomes aware of this mindset might come as the result of a surprise encounter with nature, a trauma to the body or psyche, or a pharmacological reaction, without the proper integration strategies to comprehend the experience.

1. For further reading see Holland, Julie. *Good Chemistry: The Science of Connection, from Soul to Psychedelics.* Harper Wave, 2020.

2. For further reading on the neuroscience of feeling "at one" with nature, see: Vann SD, Aggleton JP, Maguire EA. *What Does the Retrosplenial Cortex Do?* Nat Rev Neurosci. 2009 Nov. 10(11): 792–802.

Were we more familiar and intentional with this mental state, we might be quicker to call a person's first encounter of this kind by its Biblical moniker: Revelation.

When the body is in a state of Revelation, a number of other things also happen. Objects appear as they are, rather than as the heuristics that serve as shortcuts for more efficient mental processing. Instead of seeing the flag of France, for example, a mind in this state might see three tall rectangles side by side; blue on the left, red on the right, white in between. It is simply the object as it is. Thoughts also feel clear and indisputable. We often experience a multiplicity of ideas and voices in our inner dialogue, making it hard to determine which is the authentic voice or the correct course of action. In this state of Revelation, the thoughts and ideas that arise feel centered and pure, almost as if they were coming from some Great Beyond, with a confidence and authority that could feel like Scripture.

Let us call that feeling in the body "God" and the insights that were revealed "Torah." Once we have identified the experience (whatever it feels like in one's own body) and terminology of God, we can finally have a conversation about theology. British novelist Philip Pullman explains that different texts demand different attitudes from their audiences. A courtroom jurist expects to determine whether the story they are hearing is true, but not whether it is literal or metaphorical.[3] When the Torah says, "God spoke to Moses," this does not have to mean that one man named God opened his mouth and uttered words to another man named Moses. It can mean that Moses experienced this powerful state of being, mentally clear and physically attuned, and paid close attention to the ideas that arose in that mindset.

When I study my own experiences of Revelation, I strive to recreate the precise environment of the encounter in order to return to that feeling. I think back to where and when and how I first experienced that Revelation, and I call this setting "Sinai." Sinai is the details: Where was I? A particular room? Out in nature? Alone or with other people? How many people? What was the temperature? What was I wearing? What did the space smell like? Was I hungry? Had I already eaten? Was I speaking, or hearing sounds from someone else? What were the words, and what was the music? What had I been doing before I became aware of that feeling? What had I been thinking about? Did I ingest any substances that altered my brain chemistry? Which

3. Pullman and Mason, *Origin*, 68.

emotions was I feeling before this mindset settled upon me? How long did the experience last? What did I do after it ended?

The aesthetic recreation of revelatory moments is what we will call "ritual." When we perform a ritual with the right intention and all the helpful ingredients of the senses, it actually changes our nervous system and makes us feel something shift in the body. Different rituals serve different functions; some are daily practices to help us embody this state of mind as regularly as possible. These we will call "prayer." Others help us to enhance the experience of the passage of time. This is the annual holiday cycle.

But as Gillman taught, theology is contextual. Throughout the course of our lives, the dynamism of the human condition changes our relationship to these rites. Rituals that once worked consistently and reliably to recreate Divine consciousness when we were children suddenly stop working when we hit puberty; meanwhile ceremonies we could not imagine appreciating in young adulthood seem to resonate instantly when we marry or welcome children. The same is true upon our approach to death, when new embodiments of consciousness and a lifetime of cultivation invite even more profound encounters with the Divine. Since the sensory experience of our bodies changes as we move through chapters in our lives, it makes sense that the settings that helped induce that mindset also transform. A whole category of rituals is needed to help us process and mark the transitions between those chapters. Life cycle moments are just those rituals, and their religious pageantries mark for us the changing seasons of how we approach and relate to God. Our brains evolve as we age, which means the rituals we need to revisit Divine awareness evolve alongside. A *bar/bat mitzvah* is not just a coming-of-age ceremony; it is a transformation in the human nervous system, which means a transformation in the way we communicate with God. It is no wonder life cycle events are some of the most resonant and sustained rituals in all religious traditions.

Life cycle rituals mark not only the passage of time through human consciousness, but the passage of human consciousness through the course of time. Abraham Joshua Heschel and Franz Rosenzweig both understood that revelation "occurs in eternity, outside the realm of time altogether. Time, after all, is a category of human understanding that does not apply to God."[4] Looking at the experience of the human life cycle, I might offer a reversal of this paradigm: God is a category of human understanding that does not apply to Time.

---

4. Sommer, *Revelation*, 202.

During the experience of a Divine encounter, it is not uncommon to feel that time has stopped or even jumped to the past or present, such that my consciousness seems to exist in multiple places and eras at once. The course of mortal life itself is an expression of God's eternity compressed into the space-and-time-bound realm of the human experience. Ritualizing the passage of time affords us the opportunity to stand outside of that spacetime to witness it and experience the grounded awareness of (God) consciousness. In this way, God is the state of being so present in a particular moment that we, ironically, transcend the very idea of one moment.

We can look to the recent resurgence of mindfulness meditation practices in Western culture as one expression of the realignment of our bodies and awareness with what our religious traditions have long referred to as God. If the nervous system is our primary vessel for Divine communication, then intentional breathing and calming strategies are the latest fad rituals in our contemporary religious milieu. By expanding our definitions of religious language that we are accustomed to dismissing as primitive or supernatural, and by dislodging our thinking from the time-tested grooves in which we find comfort, we may discover God in ways we never thought possible. God, being a natural process built into the human genome, is available to us always and forever. Aligning the experience of God with scientific and religious language offers us a poetic framework and a set of tools that can enhance our experience of being alive. This is religion at its best.

Rami Schwartzer is an American-Israeli rabbi, teacher, and spiritual entrepreneur. He is the founder of numerous Jewish start-ups, including Ramah Day Camp Greater DC and the Den Collective. He consults on innovation and creative religious expression throughout the Jewish community.

The Holy Days

A Religious Naturalistic View

—RABBI RIFAT SONSINO

DURING THE YEAR, IT is customary to set aside a few significant days for special rituals and ceremonies. These are "holy days," and their significance can change over the centuries. The Jewish holy days are no exception. The comments below represent an attempt to reinterpret them in line with my religious naturalist philosophy.

THE SABBATH—*SHABBAT*—שבת

In Judaism, the seventh day of the week, the Sabbath, is a day of rest. The Hebrew Bible gives us two different rationales for this special day. According to Exod 20:8–11, God created the world in six days and rested on the seventh; whereas according to Deut 5:12–15, the observance of *Shabbat* is based on a humanitarian reason: "so that your male and female slave may rest as you do."

In Jewish literature, both biblical and rabbinic, *Shabbat* stands for a number of basic values: a day of rest; a sign of the covenant between God and Israel (Exod 31:17); a reminder of our commitment to freedom and justice, referred to historically as "a memorial of the Exodus from Egypt" (Deut 5:15); a day of joy (*Oneg Shabbat*) set aside for personal growth and happiness; a day of peace (*Shabbat Shalom*), and "a foretaste of the Messianic times."

Shabbat extends from sundown to sundown. On Friday evening, it is customary to light candles (a symbol of divine light and creation), to recite a blessing of sanctification (the *Kiddush*) over a cup of wine (a symbol of joy), and to say the blessing (*ha-motzi*) over the bread (symbol of life). The members of the household then share a festive meal. It is also appropriate to attend services in the synagogue on Friday evening and/or on Saturday morning.

Shabbat ends with a special service of conclusion, *Havdalah*, marking the separation of the sacred from the secular, and *Shabbat* from the rest of the days of the week. For this ceremony, a glass of wine, various spices, and a multi-wicked braided candle is used. A blessing is recited over each one.

During the Sabbath, a day of rest, no work is allowed (Exod 20:10). In fact, the Jewish Code of law, the *Mishnah*, written around 200 CE, has thirty-nine categories of forbidden acts that apply to this day (Shab. 7:2), which include items such as plowing, reaping, binding sheaves, etc.

The problem for us is how to understand the concept of rest today? Rabbinic prohibitions mostly reflect an agricultural society. Most of us, however, are not farmers, and these prohibitions do not make much sense now in an industrial society. Already, Samuel Holdheim (d. 1860), an early Reform Rabbi from Germany, had distinguished between "rest" and "sanctification," arguing that the true object of the Sabbath can be achieved only through the latter.[1] So, today, most liberal movements in Judaism struggle with the idea of how to keep the seventh day as a special day. In 1952, Israel Bettan, another Reform Rabbi and academic at the Hebrew Union College, looked favorably when someone attended a pressing community function or held public dances. For him the Sabbath should be dedicated to activities that delight the soul.[2] For us, in the 2020s, *Shabbat* represents a personal commitment and may include activities such as listening to music, visiting family or the sick, taking hikes, attending religious services, studying, going to a concert, etc., thus giving new meaning to the traditional concepts of *Kedushah* (sanctification), *Menuhah* (rest) and *Oneg* (joy of the Sabbath.)[3]

---

1. Plaut, *Rise*, 190.

2. Jacob, *American Reform Responsa*, 114–17.

3. Knobel, *Gates of the Seasons*, 21.

THE HIGH HOLY DAYS

Rosh Hashanah—ראש השנה and *Yom Kippur*—יום כפור

During the fall season, Jews celebrate two major holydays: *Rosh Ha-shanah*, the New Year, and, ten days after, *Yom Kippur*, the Day of Atonement. *Rosh Hashanah* falls on the first day of the month of *Tishri* (Sept./ Oct.) *Yom Kippur*, considered the "Sabbath of Sabbaths," falls on the tenth of *Tishri*. On the eve of *Kippur*, the congregation listens to the singing of *Kol Nidre* (pronounced as *Kal* by most Sephardic communities), "All the vows." The somber day ends the next evening with *Neilah* and *Havdalah*. Many people fast from sundown to sundown.

Rosh Hashanah is also considered a day of judgment. In the monotheistic religions of the West, namely Judaism, Christianity and Islam, there is a belief that at the end of time, God will judge all humanity, bringing the righteous to paradise and the wicked to hell. In Hebrew this is called *Yom ha-Din*—the Day of Judgment, a term that first appeared in post-biblical times. The terrifying scene of the Judgment Day has been magnificently portrayed by Michelangelo in his famous painting, The Last Judgment, now in the Sistine chapel in the Vatican.

Inspired by the Roman military, the ancient Rabbis imagined that, particularly on *Rosh Hashanah*, "all that come into the world will pass before God like legions of soldiers." (RH 1: 2). They also taught that *Rosh Hashanah* initiates a process of divine judgment that is completed on *Yom Kippur*. In fact, on *Rosh Hashanah*, they said, two books are opened before God. Some people are written in the Book of Life, while others are written in the Book of Death (see, b. RH 32b).

The theme of final judgment is highlighted in a traditional text called, *Unetane Tokef* —Let us Speak of Awesomeness, composed between the sixth and eighth centuries, and recited during the Jewish High Holidays. It states, in part, "On *Rosh Hashanah* it is inscribed, and on *Yom Kippur* it is sealed. How many shall pass away and how many shall be born? Who shall live and who shall die?" It concludes with, "But repentance, prayer, and righteousness avert judgment's severe decree."

Instead of talking about *Yom Ha-Din*, the Day of Final Judgment, I prefer to look at the High Holy Days, as an opportunity to engage in self-evaluation, which is done in the recesses of our hearts. So, we begin the process on *Rosh Hashanah*, and conclude it on *Yom Kippur*, with our new commitment to improve ourselves, thus giving a new interpretation to the traditional concept of *Teshuvah*—personal repentance. At least this is something we can do, and must do. The Talmud even gives us an example of how to do it. After death, we are told, when people are brought to judgment, they are asked: a) Did you conduct your business with integrity? b) Did you engage in procreation? c) Did you set aside times to study? and d) Did you hope for better things to come? (b. Shab. 31a).

THREE PILGRIMAGE HOLY DAYS

In biblical times, the Israelites were expected to make a pilgrimage to Jerusalem three times a year to celebrate major agricultural festivals: *Pesah*—Passover, *Shavuot*—the Feast of Weeks, and *Sukkot*—Booths. Later on, each was associated with historical events of the past.

Pesah—Passover—פסח

The festival of Passover falls on the fourteenth day of the first Hebrew month, *Nisan* (March/April). It is a combination of two festivals: *Hag ha-Pesah*—The Festival of *Pesah*, an agricultural feast characterized by the slaughter and consumption of the paschal lamb (Lev 23:5) and *Hag ha-Matzot*—the Feast of Unleavened Bread (Exod 23:15), marking the start of the grain harvest. Later on, these two were combined, historicized, and connected with the Exodus from Egypt. On the first night of Passover, during an elaborate meal, called the *Seder* (Order), Jews read/chant the *Haggadah* (the Telling), by sharing in the legendary experience of the Israelites who were slaves in Egypt and became free when they left the country in haste. During Passover fermented grain products—*hametz* are not consumed.

Even though the historical background is clouded, I choose to celebrate Passover as a festival of freedom, not only from physical bondage but also from spiritual bondage. For me, the holy day urges us to identify with the plight of people around the world who are suffering from oppression, to think of those who are victims of sexual or physical abuse, to support many who are living in poverty and squalor, and to rededicate ourselves to good works by doing our share in the redemption of all Jews and even the entire humanity.

Shavuot—Weeks—שבועות

The festival of *Shavuot* is celebrated on the sixth day of *Sivan* (May/June). In biblical times, this holy day marked the end of the barley harvest and the beginning of the wheat harvest, but, later on, when it was historicized, it was given a new interpretation, namely, the giving of the Torah at Mt. Sinai. The Bible calls the festival by different names, all related to the main function of the holy day: *Hag Shavuot*, referring to the seven weeks following Passover; *Yom Habikurim*—the Day of the Firstfruits, referring to the first products of the harvest brought by the pilgrims to the Temple of Jerusalem; *Hag Hakatzir*—the Harvest Festival, and *Zeman Matan Toratenu*—the Season of the Giving of our Torah.

Unlike Orthodox Jews and other literalists who believe that the Torah was verbally revealed on Mt. Sinai, most liberal Jews and the majority of biblical scholars today maintain that the Hebrew Bible circulated orally for many generations, and was finally written down over a long period of time. In fact, scholars today speak of four different strands that make up the Pentateuch. Instead of "revelation," I prefer to deal with the "discovery" of the marvels of nature and written texts that were produced as a result of human insights and inspiration. They articulate values worthy of living, and issues of life and death that we face every day.

Sukkot—Booths—סוכות

The festival of *Sukkot* begins on the fifteenth day of Tishri, just five days after *Kippur*. Scripture calls this festival *Hag ha-Asif*—the Festival of the Fall Harvest, *Sukkot,* or simply *He-Hag*—The Festival, par excellence. The seventh day is called *Hoshanah Rabbah*—the Great Hosanna, the following day is known as *Shemini Atzeret*—the Eighth day of Convocation, and the final day, *Simhat Torah*—the Celebration of the Torah, when the reading cycle of the Pentateuch is completed and the congregation begins with Genesis once again.

During *Sukkot*, it is customary to build a *Sukkah*, a booth, and to have at least fourteen meals in it (Suk. 2:6), in recognition of those who built a temporary abode during the Fall Harvest in biblical times. Also, during the festival, one uses four different species during religious services, waiving them in four different directions. They are the *Lulav*—the branch of a palm tree, *Etrog*—citron, *Hadas*—myrtle and *Aravah*—willow. According to some Rabbis, the *Lulav*, a masculine symbol, and the *Etrog*, representing the female breast, are combined to highlight the wholeness of humanity.[4] For other Rabbis, the *Etrog* stands for the heart, the Palm for the backbone, the Myrtle for the eyes, and the Willow for the lips. When they are combined, they symbolize our commitment to stand in awe before the miracle of existence.[5]

Sukkot was also the Pilgrims' inspiration for the first Thanksgiving in America. The festival does not have an association with a major historical event, even though the *Sukkah* reminds us of the wanderings of the Israelites who lived in primitive huts during their peregrinations in the Sinai desert (Lev 23:42).

Clearly, *Sukkot* was a festival for ancient farmers. In our time, for many of us, city dwellers, a *Sukkah*, can be viewed as a symbol of gathering for immigrants from far away countries. As a temporary structure, it can teach us to pursue equality among all people. As a fragile building, it can point to our human limitations, thus becoming a symbol of our ephemeral life. During *Sukkot*, we can rejoice over our daily occupation as successful harvests, and express gratitude for life and relationships at this traditional *Zeman Simhatenu*—Season of Rejoicing.

OTHER HOLY DAYS

Hanukkah—חנוכה

The Hebrew word *Hanukkah* means Dedication. It begins on the twenty-fifth of *Kislev* (Nov./Dec.) and lasts eight days. It is not found in the Hebrew Bible but in the First and Second Books of Maccabees in the Apocrypha. It commemorates the military victory of the Jewish rebels (the so-called Maccabees), against the Syrian-Greeks, in the second century BCE. After a few fierce battles, the Jews, under the leadership of Judah the Maccabee, defeated the enemy and rededicated the Temple of Jerusalem to the worship of one God, which had been desecrated by Antiochus IV, the king of the Syrian Greeks and his army. Each night, one lights a candle on the *Menorah*, an eight-branched candelabra. It is also customary during the festival to exchange gifts and celebrate the event with joy and jubilation.

---

4. *Sefer Sefat Emet,* on Sukkot.
5. *Sefer Hahinuh,* #285.

We do not know why the festival lasts eight days. According to a rabbinic legend, when the Maccabees entered the Temple of Jerusalem, they found a flask of oil enough for one night, but miraculously, it lasted eight (b. Shab. 21b). However, over the centuries, various explanations have been proposed, including the theory that it was a late *Sukkot*.

In our time, *Hanukkah* has assumed major importance in the world Jewish community, because it falls around December when Christians celebrate Christmas, and, more powerfully, because of its message of religious freedom. The Maccabees fought for the right to live according to their tradition. *Hanukkah* stands for the first battle in history for religious liberty.

Tu B'shvat—טו ב'שבט

The fifteenth day of the month of *Shevat* (Jan./Feb.) is designated as the New Year for the trees. Since the founding of the State of Israel, it has now assumed new meaning as a time to plant new trees, in Israel and other countries where Jews live. I would like to see it as a symbol of our firm commitment to ecological issues confronting our society, such as the preservation of forests, global warming, waste disposal, ozone depletion, overfishing and others.

Purim—פורים

The festival of *Purim* is celebrated for one day on the fourteenth of *Adar* (March/April) and in Jerusalem on the fifteenth. Based on the biblical book of Esther, it recalls the heroism of Queen Esther, the wife of king Ahasuerus, and her cousin Mordecai, against the evil plans of Haman, a royal official, who wanted to destroy the Jewish people in ancient Persia. His plans failed and the Jewish people survived. During the festival, the Book of Esther is read, and many joyful celebrations are kept at home and in the synagogue, such as fairs and carnivals. People exchange gifts and give money to charity.

The Book of Esther is not an historical text but an historical novel. Because of its message of freedom and salvation, *Purim* has spawned many local Purims, such as the *Purim* of Cairo (1323), the *Purim* of Tiberias (1743), and the *Purim* of Adrianople (1786) and others.[6] Throughout the

---

6. Deutsch, et al., *Purims, Special*, para. 1

centuries, *Purim* has come to represent the travails of Jewish communities around the globe that have survived anti-semitic attacks. The holy day also strengthens our resolve to fight for survival under difficult conditions and to celebrate the fall of evil acts carried out every day.

Yom Hashoah—Holocaust Remembrance Day—יום השואה

This holy day, which falls on the twenty-seventh of *Nisan* (April/May), marks the murder of about six million Jews by the Nazis in Germany during the Second World War. The day is a constant reminder to Jews and indeed all human beings that evil can triumph unless checked by high ethical standards. It is customary to attend special services or gatherings, by lighting memorial candles and reciting appropriate texts dealing with death and oppression.

Yom Haatzmaut—Israel's Independence Day—יום העצמאות

Celebrated with songs and festivities on the fifth of *Iyyar* (May/June), this holy day marks the founding of the modern state of Israel on May 14, 1948. The rebirth of Israel, centuries after the destruction of the Second Temple of Jerusalem in 70 CE by the Romans, and after the atrocities of the *Shoah* committed by the Germans in our time, is viewed as a symbol of hope against total despair.

Rabbi Rifat Sonsino, Ph.D., is the Rabbi Emeritus of Temple Beth Shalom, Needham, MA, and a retired academic.

Lessons I Learned From My Teacher
Ira Eisenstein's Religious Naturalism

—Rabbi Dennis C. Sasso

We Jews have been called the "People of the Book." But as much as ours is a literary tradition, it is also a tradition of teachers and mentors. We are shaped not only by text-books, but by text-people. Behind the Torah text stands *Moshe Rabenu,* "Moses, our Teacher." I have forgotten many of the things I learned during my years in formal education, but I will never forget the impact of some very special role models, preeminent among them, Rabbi Ira Eisenstein.

I studied with Ira at the Reconstructionist Rabbinical College, of which he was the founding President. Upon ordination, I was privileged to serve for three years as his associate rabbi at the Reconstructionist Synagogue of the North Shore, in Long Island, New York, until Sandy and I came to Indianapolis in 1977, to serve Congregation Beth-El Zedeck.

Ira Eisenstein was born in Harlem, New York, in 1906 and grew up in the Bronx. He studied at Columbia College and was ordained at the Jewish Theological Seminary, where he came under the intellectual and spiritual tutelage of Rabbi Mordecai Kaplan. Ira's life spanned the twentieth century and intersected with the most important personalities, events, and currents that shaped contemporary American Judaism. Ira helped to popularize and propagate Kaplan's thought and made it possible for his ideas to find practical and institutional expression in American Jewish life. Ira served as Rabbi Kaplan's associate rabbi at the Society for the Advancement of Judaism, he was editor of the *Reconstructionist,* President of the Jewish Reconstructionist Foundation, the Federation of Reconstructionist Congregations and Fellowship, and, as mentioned, the Founder and first President of the

Reconstructionist Rabbinical College. Rabbi Kaplan appropriately recognized these accomplishments in the Dedication to Ira of his book, *Not So Random Thoughts*: "To Ira Eisenstein—who is translating Reconstructionism into a not-so-random movement."[1]

But Ira's influence cannot be reduced to that of being a scholar and a movement builder. He was above all a *mensch*, a genuine human being. If his mind came under the spell of Mordecai Kaplan, it was Judith, Kaplan's daughter, who truly captured Ira's heart. Judith was a noted ethnomusicologist who taught at the School of Sacred Music of the Hebrew Union College—Jewish Institute of Religion and served as musical director at my first congregation, the Reconstructionist Synagogue of the North Shore. Ira and Judy's love nourished them for a lifetime and modeled an example for Sandy and me and so many of their disciples.

From Ira, I learned that Judaism is not an abstract idea, that religion does not exist in a vacuum, that religion is as religion does. Judaism begins with the Jewish people; religion is a human, social reality, one in which "Belonging precedes Believing." If we want to help Jews love and practice their heritage, we must first make them feel at home in the tradition and community and feel that they have a stake in it.

Eisenstein developed Kaplan's notion of Judaism as "the evolving religious civilization of the Jewish people." While religion is at the core of Judaism, it is not all there is to being a Jew. Judaism as a civilization includes a rich history, law, language, literature, music, art, rituals, folkways, social standards of conduct, spiritual ideals, and aesthetic values. Judaism is not static or monolithic; it is dynamic, culturally and ethnically diverse, and pluralistic. It is rooted in tradition, but responsive to change. The past has a vote, but not a veto.

Eisenstein challenged young rabbinical students to unlearn certain assumptions about religion. Many Jews still labor under the premodern mythic notion that God revealed the Torah to Israel. Eisenstein reversed the formulation: The people of Israel, in our search for God, create the Torah. Torah is a human document. Torah is not only a set of answers, it is a series of questions. We are not only the recipients of Torah, we are also its creators and its shapers for future generations. The Torah is holy, not because it is God's final and unchanging word, but because it is our first word, the earliest record of our people's ongoing quest for God.

---

1. Kaplan, *Not So Random*, dedication page.

Eisenstein proposes that "In the history of the Jewish people, belief in God has remained a constant, but the conception of God has varied."[2] Following an excursus of how God had been conceived supernaturally in different periods, he suggests that for the modern Jew, God should be understood in naturalistic terms, as the "Power... which makes for life, for creativity, for freedom, for peace, in short, for the fulfillment of what . . . human beings have come to recognize as the legitimate aspirations of mankind (sic)."[3]

Already Maimonides and Spinoza had taught that God is not a Being, a supernatural "somebody." Eisenstein's religious naturalism invites us to think of God as a creative process, power, or energy that animates all reality, manifesting itself at the human level as consciousness and the urge for good.

"We cannot actually picture goodness. It is not a being—it is a force, like electricity. Nobody ever actually sees electricity. We know that it exists. We get to know what electricity is by what it does. In the same way, we get to know what God is by what God makes us do...

Belief in God has to do with our attitude toward life itself. If we believe that life is worthwhile, that it is good, that, in spite of sickness and accidents, in spite of poverty and war, in spite of all the sad and difficult conditions in the world. The world is a wonderful place . . . and can be made . . . better, then we believe in God."[4]

Eisenstein was a committed Zionist, yet he believed in the importance of a vital and creative diaspora Judaism. For him, the unity and uniqueness of the Jewish people were expressed in terms of vocation rather than through the archaic language of chosenness. All peoples and faith communities should cultivate a sense of divine purpose and calling. God does not play favorites. God's universe is pluralistic, inclusive, and expansive, even as we celebrate and cultivate our unique and distinctive calling as Jews.

Ira taught about the lofty and broad issues of Jewish theology and life, but he also taught about the more mundane and basic realities of being human and being a rabbi. He wore his rabbinate quite naturally and disdained artificiality. When I was ordained, he told me that, in the course of my labors, I would receive a lot of criticism and some praise. He warned me not to allow the former to weaken my ego, nor the latter to inflate it. He

2. Eisenstein, *Judaism Under Freedom,* 35.

3. Eisenstein, *Judaism Under Freedom,* 48.

4. Eisenstein, *What We Mean,* 166, 168.

reminded his students that rabbis are perceived in ambivalent ways by their congregants. "On the one hand," he would say, "congregants want the rabbi to be apart from them. They want to respect [their] rabbi, and [so] prefer to keep a distance . . . On the other hand, they want rabbis to be regular [people] who are not standoffish. The narrow ridge which a rabbi must traverse [often] makes it very difficult to maintain equilibrium."[5]

Ira sought equilibrium in all areas; equilibrium between the professional and human dimensions of the rabbinate; equilibrium between the perceived needs of the Jewish people by rabbis as idealists, and the daily practical reality of the community of Israel, the people we serve and lead. He would say to Sandy and me, "People have it hard enough. Don't make it harder."

Like Kaplan, Eisenstein taught a new generation of American Jews that we live in two civilizations. One is our ancestral Jewish civilization—ours not merely to receive and conserve but to renew, enrich and reconstruct. The other is our American civilization—founded on the heritage and values of democracy. As modern Jews, we need to strive for an ongoing creative synthesis of the best teachings of both civilizations. A proud American, Ira was a fervent believer in what he saw as the overarching faith of America. He believed not in uncritical patriotism, but in the values of democracy as a binding spiritual force that transcends and unifies our diverse ethnic cultures, historic religious traditions, and denominations.

Ira recognized that, ". . . Religions, like other powerful forces in human life, can be good or bad; religion per se, is not necessarily beneficent in its effect upon its adherents, or upon the world."[6] Similarly, H. Richard Niebuhr would teach, "Religion makes good people better and bad people worse."[7] Ira pointed to Nazism as an ideology that came to function as a destructive "religious," blind force upon its adherents, one that sought to undermine and destroy the values of western civilization. Ira advanced the notion that, in contrast, democracy, at its best, enshrines the values that are core to our modern religious outlook. In non-supernaturalist religious terminology, democracy functions as the religious outlook and practice that makes for a godly society of freedom, justice, peace, the dignity and

---

5. Eisenstein, *Reconstructing*, 76.

6. Eisenstein, *Judaism Under Freedom*, 247.

7. H. Richard Niebuhr (1894–1962), the younger brother of Reinhold Niebuhr, is one of the most important Protestant theological ethicists of the twentieth century. He is best known for his books, *Christ and Culture* and *The Responsible Self.*

worth of the individual, and harmonious cooperation among individuals and groups.[8]

These ideas were captured in *The Faith of America*, a collection of prose and poetry, that includes readings, songs, and prayers. Taken from foundational documents and literary gems of our American democracy, they serve as fitting liturgies for the celebration of American civic holidays. Ira believed that democratic values represent religious ideals central to our individual and collective salvation. Salvation is not a supernaturalist, otherworldly experience, but the very fulfillment of our human individual and collective potential.

Until the last weeks of his life (Ira died at age ninety-four, in 2001), his disciples would visit him and study with him. He would sit at his computer and email students, family and friends. Every note, he acknowledged; every call he returned. I would often phone him to consult on matters, personal and professional.

Ira's lucidity and clarity of mind never left him. He shunned what he called the metaphysical hairsplitting to which many resort to explain God's role in light of the evil in the world. He explained, "I am not concerned about saving God's reputation for omnipotence or goodness. My theology does not call for this kind of apologetics. For me, God is the name we attach to those powers in nature and in humanity . . . which make for harmony and growth, for interdependence and self-realization, for the polar values of cooperation and individualization."[9]

Ira was a pragmatist. He lamented the fact that religion is so often muddled by unrealistic, supernaturalist concerns. In the closing paragraph of his autobiography, he affirms, "Pragmatism . . . is in disrepute . . . It has lost its original thrust. Pragmatism grew out of the spirit of activism, the intuition that an idea, to be meaningful, must be translatable into action. . . Speculation concerning ultimate things is a pleasant occupation, but there is work to be done, and that work presupposes only one affirmation about the nature of life, namely, that the potential is there. That is the simple faith on which I have based my life. I believe it is enough to carry us through even the most difficult times."[10]

Ira believed that it is incumbent upon each generation of Jews to renew the faith and to keep faith with future generations by committing

8. Eisenstein, *Judaism Under Freedom*, 249.

9. Eisenstein, *Reconstructing Judaism*, 241.

10. Eisenstein, *Reconstructing Judaism*, 242.

ourselves to the unfinished agenda of making the world a safe haven for the mind to grow, the spirit to flourish, and for all people to live secure in devotion to the pursuits of equality, freedom, justice, and peace.

———————

Dr. Dennis C. Sasso has been Senior Rabbi of Congregation Beth-El Zedeck since 1977. A native of the Republic of Panama, Rabbi Sasso descends from Spanish-Portuguese Sephardic families who settled in the Caribbean following the discovery of the Americas. Rabbi Sasso obtained his B.A. in Near Eastern and Judaic Studies at Brandeis University, an M.A. in Religion from Temple University, and was ordained at the Reconstructionist Rabbinical College in 1974. He holds a Doctorate of Ministry in Theology from Christian Theological Seminary in Indianapolis, Indiana, and is the recipient of various Doctor of Divinity Honorary degrees. He and Rabbi Sandy Eisenberg Sasso, the first woman ordained by the Reconstructionist Movement, are the first rabbinical couple in world Jewish history.

Light and Dark, Faith and Science

—Rabbi Rachel Greengrass

I HAVE A BACKGROUND in chemical engineering. For my thermodynamics final, I had to design a refrigerator using the appropriate chemicals, equations, and reactions. I received an A+.

I love science. I am fascinated by the ability we have as humans to create. From time to time I have been known to help my *B'nai Mitzvah* students with their math homework.

When people learn about my background, they often ask, How does a chemical engineer become a rabbi? As if there is a large distance to travel from scientist to spiritual leader. In terms of schooling, there is, but in terms of what is at the core, there may be no two professions that have more in common.

I went into engineering because I believed in the human capacity to create, because I looked at the world with a sense of awe, a sense of mystery and wonder—a sense of possibility. When I recognized my calling to become a rabbi, it was an easy fit, because I do look at the world with a sense of awe, a sense of mystery, wonder, and possibility.

So, I signed up for rabbinical school, a program that is five years post-graduate, took the GRE for admission (nailed the math section), and off I went.

Rabbinical school wasn't always an easy fit for me as a rational scientist. In my fourth year of rabbinical school, I was taking a Greyhound bus to visit my then fiancé, now husband, in his grad school program at Syracuse. I was spending the bus time studying. To be specific, I was learning about the *Yotzer* prayer, a prayer that Jews say every morning before reciting the morning *Sh'ma*—the maxim of our faith. In this prayer, we call God the

Creator of Light and the Creator of Darkness, the Maker of Peace, and the Creator of All Things. I had always thought this was a beautiful prayer, thanking God for all the variety in creation, for the vastness of creation. Our prayer books, in fact, title the prayer "Creation."

But that is not what I was reading. There, on the Greyhound bus, I learned that this key prayer was not merely a beautiful thank you to God, no, it was a polemic against our neighbors. This prayer borrowed its text from the prophet Isaiah, quoting God's words to Cyrus. Cyrus was the king of Persia, which at the time was grappling with Zoroastrian dualism. See, Zoroastrians believed in two gods: a god of light and goodness, and a god of darkness and evil. The prophet Isaiah tells us, no, there are not two gods, "I form the light, and create darkness; I make peace, and create evil; I the Lord do all these things."[1] The *Yotzer* prayer was a reminder that these two seeming opposites, light and dark, good and evil, can come from the same source.

Now, this made sense to me in the original context, a prophet telling a king that there is only one God and that the Zoroastrians, who were a threat, were wrong in their beliefs, but what upset me so much was the idea that we made this "put down" of another faith part of our daily prayers. What upset me was that here we are, thousands of years later, still saying this polemic against Zoroastrians! While Jews are less than 0.2% of the world population, Zoroastrians are much less. Have you ever met a Zoroastrian? So, why did we still say this prayer which was suddenly not looking like a beautiful prayer of praise for creation, but instead, it was striking me as flat-out nasty.

And I had a little breakdown . . . and so did the bus.

There I was in a broken-down Greyhound bus on the side of the highway, and I began to rethink my path. Judaism was not "jiving" with my rational mind. I had made a huge mistake. So, I took the rational approach. I had my college education to fall back on, I was a couple of months away from my Master's in Hebrew Literature, I was sure there was something else I could do.

About forty-five minutes later, I had a plan. I would finish out my Masters, drop out of rabbinical school, and I would work as a Hebrew teacher or religious school teacher until I found a career using my undergraduate degree. Having made these decisions and feeling a bit more secure, I had nothing to do but look out the window.

---

1. Isa 45:7.

It was a beautiful sunny day, dust dancing on beams of sunshine, birds chirping. In crept that feeling of connection to the world around me while simultaneously feeling small and alone, feeling at once infinite and finite—this is when I feel closest to God. This creation prayer had left me feeling wounded, but here was creation itself, giving me a sense of wonder and awe.

I was moved to do something I had never done before. I prayed for a sign. I prayed: God please send me a sign that I should continue on this path. . . And right then the engine started, the bus started moving, and I found myself back on the path I had been on an hour ago, a future rabbi on a bus studying for her finals.

Yes, I momentarily got out of my rational head and asked for something that was completely irrational and then based continuing my career path on something, more likely than not coincidental, which led me to the realization that I am not a completely rational creature.

While the dualism Isaiah fought was between light and dark, from my perspective, there is a new false dualism in our society—that is that there is science or there is faith; that one is rational or religious. I believe both come from the same source. I believe we are at once rational and spiritual, that God and science can enrich one another instead of standing at odds.

The Torah portions *Tazria/Metzora,* often read together, are particularly uncomfortable Torah portions that have to do with bodily discharges, fungus, and skin disease. Yet, they teach that those who were suffering from these afflictions should be brought to the priests. You have to wonder, why not a doctor, a healer?

I want to suggest that it has something to do with the difference between being cured and being healed. Yes, these individuals with infections were washed with soap and purified water, but that wasn't enough to heal them. To be healed, they needed someone to cater to their spirits.

In 2011, I found a lump in my right breast. I was thirty-two. I was breastfeeding. My sister, mother, and grandmother all had breast lumps and they were all benign. All this to say: I thought it was nothing. I went to the doctor, went to get a biopsy, a mammogram. I went through the entire process like it was a study, for me, as a rabbi, to understand the process that so many of my congregants go through when they get diagnosed with cancer. They, not me. The sticker they put over my nipple for the mammogram had zebra stripes. I found this hilarious. When the doctor, who was also in her thirties, who had purple fingernails and purple streaks in her hair, invited me into her office, it didn't strike me as strange. But then she told me: I had breast cancer.

Tests were run, a port was placed, I began chemotherapy, and donated my long feminine hair. Days passed, I continued to work, to be a mommy, to be a wife and daughter. Weeks went by, months.

I kept waiting. Waiting for the meaning of my illness to show itself, to explain itself. I thought I would hear the diagnosis, get upset, and after a few months, begin to appreciate life more, as many of the women I know have gone through this experience. But it wasn't happening. I was not appreciating the little things more. I was not enjoying my relationships more. In fact, nothing was really changing at all in my life except for the amount of time I was spending in doctors' offices.

I asked myself: How can this experience enable me to grow? How can I make my treatment a holy endeavor? What meaning can I make of this?

I began to read cancer book after cancer book. Maybe I was meant to share this information; speak out against insecticides, the hormones we put in our food, the chemicals we spread all over our bodies unaware. Perhaps the meaning was to use my position as rabbi to change the way we consume in our culture and change the world. But I didn't. Not because I am not passionate about these things, I am, but because I still needed healing.

Rabbis tend to be the kinds of people who want everyone to like them, which means we are always trying to show our good side. But being all good, all light—it's not real. It's also very hard to be only sunshine when you are undergoing chemo, radiation, and surgery. I had to just let that go. Start being me. I know that's said a lot, but I mean, I needed to start nourishing every aspect of me, not just the parts of me that are for other people.

That *Yotzer* prayer haunts me—God is the creator of light and dark, maker of peace, creator of evil. If God is all of these things, and we are to love God, perhaps we can love ourselves as well in all our complexity. It is that we are imperfect, that we are not black or white creatures, but gray, that makes us human and lovable.

I had a complete response to my chemotherapy, a 5.5 cm tumor completely disappeared. Science saved me. The port that was put in gave me my drugs, my breasts were replaced by implants and now I will always be partially synthetic—and for that I am grateful. I was cured, but I still was not healed. I had seen the doctor but now I needed a rabbi. I needed healing of the spirit.

BeMidbar Rabbah, an ancient collection of stories and lessons, grapples with the verse from Numbers 8 where Aaron is instructed to set up the lights of the menorah. The ancient sages ask, If God is all light, then why do we need to light lights in God's dwelling? It gives a parable to explain what is happening:

> God says, "When you set up the lamps!?" What is this like? Like a king who had a friend. The king said to him: "Know that I will dine with you (at your house). So go and prepare for me!" The friend went and prepared a layperson's couch, a layperson's lamp, and a layperson's table. When the king arrived, an entourage surrounded him on either side and a golden candelabra was in front of him. Once the friend saw all of this glory he became embarrassed and hid all that he had prepared for him since it was all of the mundane objects. The king said to him, "Did I not tell you that I would dine with you?! Why did you prepare nothing for me?" The friend responded, "I saw all of this glory that came with you and I was embarrassed and hid all that I had prepared for you because it was all of the mundane objects." The king responded to him, "I swear that I will ruin all of my implements that I brought, and because of your love I will only use yours." So the Holy One is all light, as it says, "Light resides with Him" (Dan 2:22), yet God says to Israel, "Prepare for me a candelabra and lamps."[2]

In this parable, the King is God, and we are the friend. What we have to offer is pathetic in comparison to God. And yet, God hides some of God's light so that we can have the dignity of serving God. The *Sfat Emet* teaches, "This means that from the perspective of God there is no darkness in the world, rather God hid the light in this world so that there would be a way for us to honor God to find the hidden light in the world."[3] This idea, a kabbalistic one, is that our purpose here on earth is to find sparks of light and raise them up. To light our lights, even if we self-consciously feel they are not enough.

Two years later, the *Sfat Emet* taught on the same verse:

> "One of the greatest religious problems is that people fear having a relationship with God and consequently distance themselves from God. Just as angels serve God without fear despite their lower

2. *BeMidbar Rabbah, Parshat Beha'alotkha* 15:8.
3. *Sfat Emet, BeMidbar, Parshat Beha'alotkha*, 1874.

status in comparison to God, so too human beings should walk amongst them and not be afraid of developing a relationship with God and serving God."[4]

For me, my healing came through finding and lifting sparks of light. To do this I had to explore every aspect of who I was as a mother, wife, friend, daughter, and yes, rabbi. I found light in prayer, Torah study in its broadest sense, and in loving a God that I have a hard time rationalizing. I found light in yoga and dance. I found light in allowing myself to be weak with my family, my friends, and my congregation. And I found light in helping to organize a run that raised money for women going through cancer treatment who are not blessed to have the best doctors in Miami as their congregants, a run that has become annual and has raised around a million dollars to fight breast and ovarian cancer.[5]

The rational part of me knew I was cured when I got my lab results, but I wasn't healed until I allowed every aspect of myself to be seen and my soul to be nourished. Until I actively searched out light in the darkness.

That prayer which almost changed my life back on the Greyhound because it struck me as petty, stuck with me. While its origins were somewhat distasteful, I hold onto the message that good and bad can come from the same source. That knowing that there is no light without dark reminds me that when there is darkness, there is always light to be found. And for me, the light and the dark are both evidence of God.

People say belief in a higher power is a leap of faith, that it's irrational. Yet . . . have you ever felt small, vulnerable, and lonely, yet connected to the vastness of space? Have you felt a connection to someone that went beyond words? Have you marveled at a flower's ability to undergo photosynthesis and felt that feeling of awe, of the wonder of mystery? Have you ever searched for the meaning of all this?

Perhaps, there is no dualism. Perhaps everything is connected. And perhaps, when we come to a pivotal moment, we need something, someone, some sign from the outside, even if it's completely irrational, to help us to heal, to return us to our path.

---

4. *Sfat Emet, Parshat Beha'alotkha*, 1878.
5. https://www.rocknrun.org/.

Rabbi Rachel Greengrass, M.A.R.E, M.A.H.L, R.J.E was ordained from HUC-JIR in 2008 and serves Temple Beth Am in Miami. She holds several leadership roles in the Jewish community including chair of the CCAR Resolutions Committee, serves on the URJ's Commission for Social Action, is a Rabbis Without Borders Fellow, CLI fellow, a Hartman Rabbinic Fellow, founding member of RAC-FL, iLGBTQ (the "i" is for interfaith), and is currently the President of the Rabbinical Association of Greater Miami. Rabbi Greengrass co-created an award-winning Social Justice Teen Fellowship as well as themed Shabbat services for families with young children. She has several articles featured in other published works as well as a daily blog about *daf yomi*. https://livinggreengrass.home.blog

Experiencing the Holy

A College Perspective

—Rabbi Mark S. Kram

As a college freshman in Arizona, away from my midwestern roots, I sought to recreate Jewish experiences from my home and youth. The AEPi fraternity offered me that opportunity. Gathering in my "big brother's" room, a handful of us lit *Shabbat* candles, shared a taste of *hallah*, a sip (or two!) of wine, and welcomed *Shabbat*.

To our surprise, our small private gathering morphed into something bigger. Each Friday night after dinner, a growing number of brothers began to meet in the communal room of the fraternity house prior to our Tucson weekends. Slowly but steadily, our weekly gathering grew to forty or fifty guys and their dates. The candle-lighting/welcoming *Shabbat* ceremony lasted about fifteen minutes, and it developed into something more meaningful as participants added personal, voluntary comments as the conversation circled the room.

What made this particular experience meaningful enough to draw a large group of students weekly?

One reason was that it was an organic experience, owned by us. Simple and homemade, it only required us to be with friends and to connect to something we missed from home. At the same time, it connected us to something larger than ourselves.

It was never forcefully religious, and it was gentle. It did not conflict with weekend plans. There were no theological expectations or conversations (those happened at other times), and no written prayers or prayerbooks. Most importantly, there were no expectations, other agendas (written or unwritten), or goals. We were there to share something sweet and homegrown in a comfortable space. It was easy to relate to and our choice.

Another experience with college students, years later, surprised me as well. I was now a Hillel director. One Friday night, while visiting a campus that I worked with, the students and staff were ushering in *Shabbat* by a beautiful lake. (Okay, with lots of alligators!) I was given the role to offer the *Erev Shabbat* blessing that parents traditionally bestow upon their own children. We announced that this would take place, and that those who wished to receive the blessing could gather around me and my wife (also a Hillel professional). To our surprise and amazement, we were surrounded by a huge crowd of Jewish students, keen to receive this blessing.

These experiences taught me two lessons. First, when there is something that reminds students of home, even a little, and they can choose that option without any expectations or "shoulds," Jewish college students will welcome it. Second, that there is something powerful about receiving a blessing—perhaps because it was not from their own parents!

I suppose, also, that the prayers addressed student's core concerns, particularly the challenges they faced during their college years. Not the theology of Judaism, but rather the fundamental and personal issues they struggled with during their most formative years, i.e., missing home, struggling to find their way in this new [campus] world, choosing a future path, and living in an unfamiliar environment with others who challenged the views they brought with them.

College is the time to challenge youthful assumptions carried from home. It is the time to seek meaning in new ways where different people, teachers, ideas, and beliefs abound. It is the time to evaluate, encounter, and experiment. And it may also be the time to take a fresh look at the prescribed liturgy of the prayerbook, and the Judaism they grew up with.

What IS meaningful to students is absolute and unvarnished honesty, openness, and integrity. If there is any time in which to challenge conventions, this is it! The campus experience encourages questioning, testing, and trying on new beliefs for size. Authenticity, that which is genuine and real, sticks.

On campus, students *are* Israel—the people who struggle with the idea of God (and Judaism) in order to determine their own ideas of who they are and where they belong. The question of whether or not there exists a Divine Being, and if so, could that Being play a role in their Jewish lives is only one of the scores of questions they will wrestle with during their time at the academy.

To be accepted, the language of prayer must likewise be honest, authentic, genuine, and realistic. The traditional prayerbook's characterization of God as being able to change the course of history, or personally bring healing to those who are ill, will not fly. Portraying the heroes of the Torah as truly human with struggles as we each have in our lives, works. Portraying a Divine Being during prayer with powers and influence that border the magical or miraculous rather than the mysterious or unexplained, is ineffective.

In his book, *Man is not Alone* (1951), Rabbi Abraham Joshua Heschel addresses the idea of wonder. He writes that wonder is "the state of our being asked."[1] Cultivating an attitude towards life and an appreciation of the world in which wonder plays an important role can be meaningful to college students.

College students also like to celebrate and be entertained. Heschel spoke of the difference between them:

"Celebration is an active state, an act of expressing reverence or appreciation. To be entertained is a passive state—it is to receive pleasure afforded by an amusing act or a spectacle. Entertainment is a diversion, a distraction . . . from the preoccupations of daily living. Celebration is a confrontation, giving attention to the transcendent meaning of one's actions. . . To celebrate is to share in a greater joy, to participate in an eternal drama."[2]

On the campus, to speak frankly with Jewish students, one can use this language of confrontation, of experiencing, of authentically and meaningfully inviting the idea of amazement and wonder into the conversation. Prayer for these students, whether sitting around informally in a fraternity house and lighting candles, choosing to be blessed by someone else's parents, or incorporating Heschel's insights, can transform their college experience. It can raise them up, even briefly, to experience something that

1. Heschel, *Essential Writings*, 69.
2. Heschel, *Who Is Man?*, 117.

is very real. It can provide a direct and personal touch-point to something in their tradition and in their past.

Possibly something new—simple, honest, and understandable.

Rabbi Mark S. Kram, MBA, DD was ordained at HUC-JIR (C '78). He served as a Hillel professional on college campuses and as the state executive director of Hillel in Florida as well as congregations in Miami, Florida. He is Rabbi Emeritus of Temple Beth Or, Miami, Florida. He earned an MBA and continues to work as an executive coach for business and non-profit clients. He was also trained as a family mediator. He and his wife, Mindy, recently moved to North Carolina. They have three married children and, to date, four grandchildren.

What About Death?

—Rabbi Simeon J. Maslin

The ultimate question, the question that no one in the thousands of years of accumulated human wisdom has been able to answer: What about death? Here is the way that a distinguished Episcopalian priest, Walter Russel Bowie, addressed it almost a century ago:

> "What sense can be made out of existence if rocks and earth and the dust beneath our feet go on enduring and human souls, which seem to be the fruition toward which all the slow forces of evolution have been working, should blindly and stupidly be brought to naught? In the face of such a universe, one might laugh with contempt before going to annihilation. . ."[1]

One can hear frustration and anger in these words, and understandably so. It is the anger that was expressed so powerfully by Dylan Thomas' *"Do not go gentle into that good night... Rage, rage against the dying of the light."* Yes, we can rage; we can cry out in frustration; we can shake a fist at heaven, but . . . futility. We must all die, and no one has ever defeated death. And so let's start there, with those stories about characters who are *supposed* to have defeated or returned from death.

Among the Babylonians, as recounted in the Gilgamesh Epic, it was the god Tammuz who was brought back to life by Ishtar. The Egyptians told of Osiris who was resurrected by Isis. For the Greeks, it was Persephone, carried away to the netherworld by Hades and resurrected each spring through the tears of her mother, Demeter. The Norse told about Baldur and the Aztecs about Quetzalcoatl. According to Carl Jung, these ubiquitous

---

1. Greenberg, *Treasury of Comfort*, 105.

myths of resurrected pagan gods foreshadowed the story that lies at the heart of Christianity, the resurrection of Jesus.

While the Christian resurrection story, celebrated for almost two millennia each year on Easter when churches display banners proclaiming "He is risen," was certainly influenced by pagan mythology, there was also considerable support in the teachings of the first- and second-century rabbis. They may have rejected the claim that a particular itinerant preacher from Galilee did actually rise from the dead, but they injected into Judaism the idea that death is a temporary state and that God will bring the dead back to life. These early rabbis established the belief in *t'hiyat ha-metim* (restoring the dead to life, i.e. resurrection) as one of the central doctrines of Judaism:

> All of Israel has a portion in the world to come, as it is said: "And Thy people are all righteous; at the End, they shall inherit the land. . ." (Isa 60:2) But the following have no portion in the world to come; one who says that there is no resurrection of the dead and one who denies the divine authorship of the Torah. . .[2]

So essential was this belief in bodily resurrection to the early rabbis that they equated it with the axiomatic belief that God was the source of the Torah, and they included it in the liturgy that they prescribed for daily worship, especially in the second of the eighteen benedictions of the *Amidah*:

> You sustain the living with lovingkindness, revive the dead with great mercy, …. and keep faith with those who sleep in the dust…. You are faithful in granting eternal life to the dead. Blessed are You who resurrects the dead.[3]/

There were those who disagreed with the early rabbis, most notably the Sadducees who would not accept any tenet which wasn't stated specifically in the Bible, but there were also sociological reasons for their denial of resurrection. Most of the early rabbis came from the ranks of ordinary people; they had to work for their livings, and they were victims, as were all ordinary Judeans during the first three centuries of the common era, of the cruel often murderous regime of the Romans. They were, for the most part, the Pharisees. The Sadducees, on the other hand, were the priestly class and the gentry, often working hand-in-hand with the Romans. They were not subject to the same sufferings that typified the lives of ordinary Judeans.

---

2. m. San. 10.

3. Every traditional Jewish prayerbook

One can readily understand why a second-century Jew might ask one of the learned rabbis why they should observe the myriad of *mitzvot* ordained by the Torah if their Jewish observances subjected them to the cruel lash of the Romans. And so was born the concept of *t'hiyat ha-metim*. You may be suffering in this world, the rabbi would reply, but that suffering will be rewarded in the next world, in the *Olam Ha-Emet*—the real world. One of those second-century sages, Rabbi Jacob, representing the Pharisaic belief, put it quite succinctly:

> This world is like a foyer leading to the world to come. Prepare yourself in the foyer so that you may be allowed to enter the great hall.[4]

Rabbi Jacob continued his lesson by referring to the period after death as "*blissfulness of spirit in the world to come.*"

Now, those rabbis would not have had the temerity to invent the idea of life after death out of whole cloth; they needed some biblical underpinning. But while there is certainly no clearly spelled out doctrine of resurrection anywhere in the Bible, there are several verses that might be taken to support the idea. A few examples:

> "*Adonai* kills and gives life; brings down to *Sheol* and brings up." [1 Sam 2:6]

> "*Adonai*, You have brought me up from *Sheol*. . ." [Ps 30:4]

> "Many of them that sleep in the dust of the earth shall awake, some to everlasting life and some to reproaches. . ." [Dan 12:2]

But overwhelmingly, the biblical authors saw death as the absolute end of life. The poignant lament of Job is an accurate representation of the biblical view of death:

> "Remember, my life is but a breath of wind; I shall never again see good days. You will behold me no more; under your very eyes, I shall disappear. As clouds break up and disperse, so one who goes down to *Sheol* never comes back; he never returns home again, and his place will know him no more.[5]

> Shakespeare put what should be the final word on the subject into Hamlet's soliloquy:

---

4. *Pirke Avot* 4:21.

5. Job 7:7–9.

"...death, the undiscovered country from whose bourn no traveler returns."[6]

But, of course, that is not the final word. A major part of religious faith—Jewish, Christian, and Islamic—since the days of the early rabbis, has concerned itself with what happens to a person after death. I am not referring here to the question of resurrection, actually emerging from the grave and resuming animated life. What I am referring to is the belief that after death the person is transported to a place of purgation and/or reward. That belief, in its various forms, is common to all three of the Western religions and is derived from early mythologies.

In the Babylonian *Gilgamesh Epic,* the netherworld is depicted as:

> "... the land of no return ... the dark house ... the house which none leave ... the house in which the entrants are deprived of light, where dust is their fare ... and clay their food, where they see no light, residing in darkness. .."[7]

And there are similar descriptions of the place to which the dead are consigned in virtually all of the early Western mythologies.

Jewish tradition, since the period of the early rabbis, has taught that the dead are judged by a heavenly tribunal and are consigned either to *Gan Eden* (Paradise, literally the "Garden of Eden") or to *Gehinnom.* (*Gehinnom* is derived from *Ge Hinnom*—the Valley of Hinnom where the rite of child sacrifice through fire was practiced in the sixth and seventh centuries BCE.) That tradition, with numerous citations in the Talmud, the Midrash, and especially in medieval folklore, is replete with graphic descriptions of the sufferings of sinners after death.

In the tractate *Rosh HaShanah* of the Babylonian Talmud, there are two passages that describe the early Pharisaic understanding of what happens after death:

> "Sinners of Israel who sin with their bodies and sinners of the Gentiles who sin with their bodies go down to *Gehinnom* and are punished there for twelve months. After twelve months their bodies are consumed and their souls are burnt and the wind scatters them under the soles of the righteous, as it says, [Mal 3:2] "And you shall tread down the wicked, and they shall be as ashes under the soles of your feet." For those who rejected the Torah

6. Shakespeare, *Hamlet,* 3:47.
7. Pritchard, ANET, 107.

and denied the resurrection of the dead and sinned and made the masses sin, they will go down to Gehinnom and be punished there for all generations, as it says, [Isa 66:24] "They shall go forth and gaze at the corpses of the men who have rebelled against Me. Their worms shall not die nor their fire be quenched; they shall be a horror to all flesh."[8]

The School of Shammai taught: There will be three groups at the Day of Judgment—one of the thoroughly righteous, one of the thoroughly wicked, and one of the intermediate. The thoroughly righteous will be definitely inscribed as entitled to everlasting life; the thoroughly wicked will be definitely inscribed as doomed to Gehinnom. The intermediates will go down to Gehinnom and shriek and rise again, as it says, [Zech 13:9] "I will bring the third part through the fire and will refine them as silver is refined…"[9]

As indicated in the former passage, purgation in Gehinnom was thought to last for only twelve months.

Rabbi Akiba taught: The punishment for the [wicked] generation of the flood was twelve months; the punishment for Job [who questioned God] was for twelve months; the punishment for the Egyptians was twelve months; the punishment for Gog and Magog (kings who will fight against Israel at the end of time) will be for twelve months; the punishment for sinners in Gehinnom will be for twelve months. . ." [10]

Rabbi Akiba went on to offer a rather far-fetched biblical source for the belief that all who have sinned during their lifetimes will suffer purgation for twelve months, but far-fetched or not, this teaching by one of the most eminent second-century sages has persisted in Judaism to our very day. It explains why the children of deceased parents recite the Kaddish (the prayer for the souls of the dead; see below) for eleven months. For if they were to recite it for a full twelve months, they would be indicating that their parents were so wicked that they deserved the full twelve-month purgation. If this sounds silly to the modern ear, you're right; it is!

The preeminent Jewish philosopher of the Middle Ages, the rationalist Moses Maimonides, was clearly embarrassed by the graphic descriptions of the fleshly torments of Gehinnom, but there was no way that he could

8. b. RH 17a.
9. b. RH 16b.
10. Edu. 2:10.

deny what the authoritative sages of the *Mishnah* had posited as a fundamental principle of Judaism. And so, he incorporated the belief in reward and punishment and the belief in the revival of the dead as the eleventh and final of his *Thirteen Principles of Faith*. But he made it very clear elsewhere that it was the souls and not the bodies of the dead that were punished or rewarded.

What does, or did, Christianity teach about the fate of the dead? One of the best-known of those teachings may be found in the Gospel of Mark. (It should be noted that most Christian Bible translations use the word Hell as the translation for *Gehinnom*.)

> If your hand is your undoing, cut it off; it is better for you to enter into life maimed than to keep both hands and go to hell and the unquenchable fire. And if your foot is your undoing, cut it off; it is better to enter into life a cripple than to keep both your feet and be thrown into hell. And if it is your eye, tear it out; it is better to enter into the kingdom of God with one eye than to keep both eyes and be thrown into hell; Where the devouring worm never dies and the fire is not quenched.[11]

Granted that Mark (as well as a similar passage in Matthew) was employing hyperbole to make his point, but his point was that sinners are punished with the torments of Hell (or *Gehinnom*), which is exactly what the Pharisaic sages were teaching at the time. (How ironic that the Christian Bible, which so often condemns the Pharisees, is full of Pharisaic teachings!)

Just two more New Testament texts on post-mortem purgation:

> "Do not fear those who kill the body but cannot kill the soul. Fear him rather who is able to destroy both soul and body in Hell."[12]
> "The rich man also died and was buried, and in Hades, where he was in torment, he looked up; and there, far away, was Abraham with Lazarus close beside him. "Abraham, my father," he called out, "take pity on me! Send Lazarus to dip the tip of his finger in water, to cool my tongue, for I am in agony in this fire."[13]

This last text goes on to explain that Abraham and Lazarus could not help the rich man in Hades, because "there is a great chasm fixed between

---

11. Mark 9:43–48.
12. Matt 10:28, Luke 12:4–5.
13. Luke 16:22–24.

us; no one . . . can cross it." Here we have the foreshadowing of the geography of Hell that was detailed centuries later by Dante.

About half a millennium after the writings of the early rabbis and the Gospel writers on the punishments that await the sinner after death, Islam was born and incorporated that article of faith into the Qur'an. The place of punishment in the Qur'an is called *Jahannam*, obviously derived from the *Gehinnom* of early Jewish and Christian texts. References to the punishments that sinners will suffer are found throughout the Qur'an. This one is clearly derived from the Luke passage above:

> "And the companions of the Fire [*al-nar*] will call to the companions of Paradise, 'Pour upon us some water or from whatever Allah has provided you.' They will say, "Indeed, Allah has forbidden them both to the disbelievers."[14]

The Qur'an speaks of the seven levels of *Jahannam* and gives names to its different gates, again anticipating Dante's topography. And so now we skip ahead about six centuries to Dante. Inspired by the writings of Thomas Aquinas, Dante Alighieri, a fourteenth-century Italian, composed what is widely considered to be the greatest work of Italian literature, *The Divine Comedy*. In magnificent poetry, Dante described his travels through the several levels of the abode of the dead, the Inferno, Purgatory, and Paradise. He is guided through the netherworld by Virgil and through Paradise by his beloved Beatrice. He describes in detail the punishments suffered by various groups of sinners in the Inferno, for example: gluttons are forced to lie in vile slush; heretics lie in fiery tombs; the treacherous are frozen in an icy lake; fortune-tellers walk around with their heads on backward for falsely predicting the future; and so on.

What is the point of all of the above recounting of the systems of reward and punishment in the afterlife as described in pagan mythology, in the writings of the early rabbis, the Gospels, and the Qur'an? The point is that all of those descriptions stem from early mythology and were later incorporated into the canons of the Western religions. No one, ancient or modern, knows anything about what happens to the body or the soul of the deceased. There is a common psychological need to believe in ultimate justice. Evil *must* be punished, and righteousness *must* be rewarded.

But the astute observer knows from everything that he/she sees in life that this is not always the case. Ah, but it *must* be true, and so we return to

---

14. *Qur'an* 17:50.

the *Mishnah Avot*: "This life is like a foyer leading into the world to come.
. ." The only way that the ancient mind could justify the disparity between
the powerful and the meek, between the sinners and the righteous, was to
envision what the early rabbis called the *Olam ha-Emet*—the Real World,
i.e., a place of reward and punishment after death. But . . .

The fact that this other world is described in detail in some of the
most beautiful poetic imagery conceived by the human mind does not
make it true. Rabbis, priests, imams, and other religious functionaries have
been preaching about reward and punishment after death, about Hell and
Paradise, for centuries. Waving their Bibles or Qur'ans and shouting their
warnings with the deepest conviction and certainty, they have successfully
planted this article of faith into the psyches of billions of people. The pearly
gates, the forty virgins waiting for jihadists, the devil and angels with fleecy
wings—all of these images have been sold as truths for centuries. They are
as much a part of the human consciousness as a toothache. What is actually the truth? The truth is that we know nothing about what may or may
not happen after death. We know nothing, absolutely nothing, about "the
undiscovered country from whose bourn no traveler returns."

But is there anything that we *do* know? Yes, we know what modern science
has proven beyond a doubt, and that is that our DNA is immortal. There
are traces of our ancient forebears in every one of us, and not only in our
physiognomies. The stamp of our parents and their parents is evident in
our intellect, in our attitudes, in our likes and dislikes, and, for better or for
worse, in everything that we are and that we do. That is not to say that our
lives are predetermined by our genes. . . Every human being is endowed
with the genetic material of previous generations, but every human being is
also endowed with the ability to choose.

There is an essential teaching in the Passover *Haggadah*, that goes
back to the earliest rabbis. At the climactic moment of the service, before
the traditional meal, the text reads: "In every generation, a person is required to think of him/herself as if personally freed from Egypt." The idea
that we, living today, were there with the generation of Moses and the freed
slaves is reiterated in the book of Deuteronomy where Moses addressed not
only those of his generation, ". . . But also with those who are not with us
this day." [Deut 29:14] Through the genes that we inherited, *we* were slaves

in Egypt; *we* stood at Sinai; *we* sat in the academies of Hillel and Akiba. All of this is in our DNA; we are immortal.

We opened this discussion of death by quoting a few lines from a meditation by the Episcopalian priest, Walter Russel Bowie. Bowie spoke of rocks and dust enduring eternally while human beings are stupidly "brought to naught." Faced with this reality, one "might laugh with contempt before he went to his annihilation." Then Bowie continues:

> ". . . But we cannot believe that contemptuous laughter is the ultimate verdict to be passed upon our world. There must be in it something that has caused our own ideals, something akin to our passion for continuing life, and something upon which we can rely. God must be in it, and God is life, and God is love. Even in the moments when our intellect is baffled, and even in those times when contradictions beset our faith, still, we refuse to be put to permanent intellectual and spiritual confusion, and still, our deepest souls declare that beyond the shadows there is light, and in the depths of the utmost darkness life goes upon its undefeated way."

"God must be in it. . . " Here we return to our first consideration: What about God? How is God, the Infinite Intelligence who transcends the daily affairs of human beings, involved in the deaths of our mothers and fathers, our husbands and wives, our loved ones, and the homeless derelict sleeping on the sidewalk? How is God involved in our own deaths?

When the mind of God created our world and the organisms that would evolve into *homo sapiens* billions of years ago, that infinite mind created genetic codes that would evolve along with their carriers and that would survive through all the generations from the primordial ooze to you and me today. Our ideals, our intellect, and our passions were latent in the earliest organism that emerged from that ooze. That evolutionary spiral was designed by God, the God who is the source of life, the God who is infinitely beyond human understanding, the God whose love makes it possible for us to continue the search of Moses, Spinoza, and Einstein. That is our immortality, not a netherworld barbecue and not a heavenly fairyland, but the innate assurance that the evolutionary process is eternal and that a part of us will one day explore the far reaches of infinity.

Rabbi Simeon J. Maslin was Rabbi Emeritus, Congregation Keneseth Israel in Philadelphia, and a past president of the Central Conference of American Rabbis (1995–7). He died in 2022, shortly before this volume was completed.

This essay was originally published in *God for Grown-Ups; a Jewish Perspective*, by Simeon J. Maslin, Xlibris, 2019. It is included here with the author's permission.

Life Goes On . . . and On

—Rabbi Howard O. Laibson

BIG BANG

How did we all come to be? How will we all end up? These are two of those "big questions" that people rarely think about except at occasional social gatherings and in synagogue adult education courses. The Bible and Jewish mystics put forth theories that are God-centric. I don't have a problem with that generally, though my approach is different. Since this is a book about Jewish religious naturalism, I begin with science. The perspective of physicists and cosmologists is that at one moment approximately fourteen billion years ago, an infinitesimal area of energy became extremely compressed and dense until the pressure was so great that the energy burst forth in every direction. Eventually, some of that energy cooled and became material, and in innumerable locations was drawn together into communities of matter and energy, ultimately coalescing into the universe as we know it. This initial event became known as the Big Bang. It is interesting to note that this phrase was originally used in a highly derogatory manner in 1950, by British astronomer Fred Hoyle,[1] who thought the concept lacked credibility. But the label stuck and today, the Big Bang is generally accepted by the scientific community as the beginning of everything.

While I embrace the results of physical science, I nonetheless believe, teach and preach the importance of spirituality in our lives. Along these lines, I insert the role of God into the process of the Big Bang. For me, God is the Divine Purposive Energy that began creation with the Big Bang

1. Nelson, *Judaism, Physics and God*, 4.

and that drives all living creatures to live, survive, and when circumstances permit it, to thrive. God is the energy that powers life-sustaining processes.

Let's examine the role of energy after the Big Bang.

Professor Daniel Matt reminds us that, following the dramatic explosion of energy, "time and space began. But the early universe was an undifferentiated blend of energy and matter. How did matter emerge?

> "A scientist would say that the energy congealed. Matter is frozen energy. No nucleus or atom could form until some energy cooled down sufficiently that it could be bound and bundled into stable particles of matter.
>
> "Einstein discovered the equivalence of mass and energy. Ultimately, matter is not distinct from energy, but simply energy that has temporarily assumed a particular pattern. Matter is energy in a tangible form; both are different states of a single continuum, different names for two forms of the same thing."

Dr. Matt adds, and as a religionist, I assert: "Divine energy pervades all material existence."[2] Professor Richard Elliott Friedman similarly states, "Some remnant of the divine light that burst in at the moment of the expansion persists. There is a residue of divine manifestation in every being."[3] Those sparks of divine energy are part and parcel of everything—animate and inanimate.

In other words, the collections of energy and matter that emerged from the Big Bang are all reflections of their source, God. All of these collections, and everything that grew out of them, everything that evolved from them, remain reflections or extensions of God.

In the well-worn path of evolution on this planet, we began with single-celled bacteria and, over a vast amount of time, we saw the development of plants, hundreds of species of insects, all sorts of animals, and ultimately arrived at the emergence of human beings. It would be hubris to assume that we are the final stage of that evolutionary path. But for now, we are at the top rung of the evolutionary ladder. As we observe this entire evolutionary process, we can readily discern its purpose—LIFE.

From a spiritual perspective, it is important to know in this connection that the most frequently mentioned name of God in the Bible is *YHVH*, which means "the One who causes to be." God brings everything into being, through the explosive Big Bang and the perpetual growth of evolution.

2. Matt, *God and the Big Bang*, 44.
3. Friedman, *Hidden Face*, 229.

The result is, eventually, the emergence of a vast array of species of living things. Surely, this is the purpose behind God's emanation of divine energy. Professor Daniel Matt indicates: "If God spoke the world into being [as the Bible indicates], the divine language is energy; the alphabet, elementary particles; God's grammar, the laws of nature."[4]

END OF LIFE

This brief sketch summarizes where we have all come from cosmically and biologically. Let's now examine how we will all end up. The more specific question is, "What happens when we die?" From a strictly scientific perspective, the answer is rather clear. When we die, our biological functions of respiration and neural activity shut down. Our heart stops beating, our lungs no longer operate, so blood no longer feeds the body with oxygen, the brain ceases functioning, and we are dead. That is the end. This may not be a happy ending, but as far as science is concerned, that is the basic truth. We all die.

It won't surprise the reader to know that this perspective, that biological death is the final end, was not satisfactory to our ancient religious leaders. Judaism has espoused several approaches to the afterlife. Many biblical references state that the dead go down to *Sheol*, generally understood to be some sort of dark pit under the earth.[5] At King Saul's demand, the witch of *En Dor* even brought the prophet Samuel back from there, much to his displeasure.[6] And the Book of Daniel speaks of a time when the dead will awaken, some to everlasting life, others to everlasting rejection.[7]

The earliest generations of Rabbis expanded this theme into a rather elaborate scheme that has several components. Let me summarize them.[8] After death, a person's soul returns to God and endures a period of purifying punishment. The best metaphor I can think of to describe the value of this experience is psychotherapy. In psychotherapy, we undergo a process of reviewing those memories, experiences, and choices which have made us who we are. This often involves examining past conflicts, wounds and scars, and other painful sources of our stunted personal and spiritual growth.

---

4. Matt, *God and the Big Bang*, 28.

5. See Gen 37:35; 42:38; Num 16:30; Ezek 31:14; Ps 88:7, 13; Lam 3:55; many others.

6. 1 Sam 28:13–15.

7. Dan 12:2.

8. Borowitz, *Liberal Judaism*, 214–15.

While the process is sometimes emotionally trying, it is ultimately growth-inducing. We are better people for it.

So, too, are our souls fully grown resulting from the process of purification the Rabbis understood to occur following death. Our souls then dwell in the *Olam HaBa*, the World to Come. While the Rabbis developed some fanciful ways of describing the *Olam HaBa*, I do not find them to be compelling. Let me say directly, no one really knows what the afterlife is like, except that it is some sort of personal survival after the body ceases to function.

The Rabbis indicated, as well, a continuation of the process, and here I disagree with them. They taught that, once the Messiah comes, all souls are reunited with their bodies, which will have arisen from the grave. Each resurrected person, then, stands before God for a final judgment. The righteous then live forever, embodied. The rest are denied eternal life for up to twelve months.[9]

I find this whole issue of bodily resurrection (which Christianity borrowed from Jewish sources) to be beyond the realm of serious consideration. The concept is simply too fantastic, in the literal sense of that term. I cannot conceive of a process where dust can be re-formed into muscle, bone, sinew, and skin, and then rise up out of the ground. While I can grasp that the process of decay can be slowed, I don't know how it can be reversed. My understanding of God excludes breaking the laws of nature. However, this should not preclude the survival of the soul.

So, how does this view of a Jewish afterlife (there are others, by the way, but that would take us beyond the scope of this essay) compute with the concept of God as the energy which powers life-sustaining processes?

Fascinatingly, the Rabbis referred to God's felt Presence as the *Shekhinah*. Jewish mystics viewed the *Shekhinah* as a surging, fiery source of energy,[10] reaching out invisibly to each and every one of us in the womb, implanting within us, and animating us, with a "spark of divinity." The "spark of the divine" is usually understood metaphorically. I view it *literally*.

What do we know about energy? We know that the absence of energy pulsing throughout our nervous system is rapidly becoming the authoritative factor that determines death has occurred. When our brains no longer register a response from an EEG machine, we are considered deceased. This is known as "brain death."

9. *Pirke Avot* 4:28; *Eduyot* 2:10; Sonsino and Syme, *What Happens*, 25–30.

10. Rashi on Gen 15:10:1; Rabbenu Bahya, Exod 33:13:8; *Akedat Yitzhak* 54:1:14.

We also know that generally, energy tends to travel along the lines of least resistance. Thus electrical currents move along pathways of neurons. A substance known as myelin forms along neural pathways that are habitual, essentially "greasing" the path of specific patterns of energy flow.

How does this play out in terms of human experience? Not to be overly reductionistic, but in what we call *personality*. Each of us utilizes our energy in ways that are unique and habitual. Based on our human experience, our thinking, feeling, and behaving form a characteristic pattern that accounts for our particular habits, our typical styles of response, our individuality. Thus our energy flows in a characteristic way.

What else do we know about energy? We know that it can never be destroyed. What happens, then, when we die? What happens to the divine energy within us? If it cannot be destroyed, if it never ceases, where does this life force go when our body ceases functioning? I cannot help but believe that somehow, something of each person's individuality—in its most *soulful*, energetic common denominator—continues to maintain its patterned ways, living on . . . and on. . . . I don't pretend to know how, or where. But it is reasonable to believe that it does.

I believe that our life experience is truly something grand and mysterious. Our lives are typically played out in the most naturalistic and largely empirically verifiable mechanisms. But there is a part of that process that is unknown to us, and very probably is unknowable. That's where the mystery comes in. I am convinced that life is much more than, as one behaviorist put it, "muscle twitches and gland squirts." I further believe that there is within each of us real Godliness, which powers us, which gives us life, which energizes us to live fully, and with which we are inextricably intertwined.

I believe that Judaism offers something to us which is genuinely redemptive, even in this sometimes cynical, post-modern time of ours. Life is occasionally joyous, too often unfulfilling, or even unkind. Judaism reasonably suggests the possibility that there is a meaning to it all which transcends this life. How amazing this is! How comforting! For if God is Eternal, which I consider axiomatic, and Divine energy has powered us, then how can we *not* have a share in God's Eternality?

––––––––––

Rabbi Howard O. Laibson is Rabbi Emeritus of Congregation Shir Chadash of Lakewood, CA. He was ordained as a rabbi in 1981, earned an M.A. in

Education/Counseling in 1975 and a Master of Hebrew Letters in 1979. He spent the entirety of his professional career serving the Jewish people in congregations.

Is There a Righteous Judge?

Notes on Funeral Liturgy

—Edmond H. Weiss

From the Stoics to the present, philosophers have urged us to manage our fear of death by not thinking about it. Julian Barnes' book on the subject is called *Nothing to be Frightened Of*, and the double meaning in the title lays out the whole problem. There is nothing in death that should frighten us, because the dead experience nothing. But, at the same time, the idea of eternal nothingness is terrifying, even though all of us experienced it for the fourteen billion years before we were born.

Some argue that the "denial of death" is a prime motivator for religion itself. Nearly all the world's religions provide either for an afterlife, a reincarnation, a resurrection, or some other alternative to endless oblivion. And, typically, they frame this alternative as a reward for obedience. The Jewish idea of an *olam haba*, a world to come, arrives relatively late in the formation of the religion and it serves not only as an alternative to oblivion and a reward for observing the commandments, but also as a way for the God of Israel to fulfill the covenantal promises he failed to fulfill during the lives of the original Israelites.

It is possible, however, to make small changes in the supernatural Jewish funeral liturgy that can moderate our thinking about death and help ease us into a more naturalistic understanding of the end of life.

Baruh Dayyan HaEmet—ברוך דיין האמת

Although it is the shortest of the Blessings (only three words), it is fraught with theological and philosophical problems.

It was once spoken by Jews after any terrible event, but today's Jews are enjoined to say it either upon observing, or learning of, a person's death. Also, at the beginning of a funeral service, the rabbi gathers the family of the deceased, cuts or tears the black memorial ribbons pinned to their clothes, and has them repeat—often one word at a time for those who have not spoken Hebrew in a while—*Baruh, Dayan, HaEmet*: Blessed is the Righteous Judge.

Built into this heavy little sentence is a compressed version of the entire supernatural *Yom Kippur* liturgy. The moment of our death is not merely the conclusion of a natural process or catastrophic event. It is, rather, a death sentence imposed by a brilliant jurist who knows all our deeds and has determined that our flaws and ethical shortcomings deserve this ultimate resolution. The moment and manner of the death, moreover, may have been adjudicated long ago.

Even though there are very few *mitzvot*—commandments that promise longer life to the observant (honoring one's parents and using honest weights are among them), the sages make it clear that we all die for a reason. For example, the commentary on the death of Sarah asks why she did not live as long as Abraham. *Genesis Rabbah* speculates that Sarah should have reached Abraham's age of 175 years, but forty-eight years were taken away because of her readiness to dispute with Abraham over Hagar. It seems that her years were reduced when she said, "Let *Adonai* judge between you and me."[1] The Talmud teaches that "Whoever plunges early into litigation does not escape from it unscathed."[2]

My experience with dying and funerals has led me to think of this blessing as one offered grudgingly or ironically. Although much is made of the fact that the Mourners' *Kaddish* does not mention death, the righteous judge claim refers not only to the death of someone we cared for but even suggests strongly that he or she had it coming. Taken seriously, it is a galling thing to say upon the loss of someone we loved, especially if that death was premature or tragic.

---

1. Gen 16:5.
2. b. B. Kam. 93a.

Given this kind of thinking, it is even possible to blame the ancestors of the deceased, because the sins of parents may have been "visited" down through the generations.

And should mourners express anger or protest, should the unfairness of the situation bring out a bit of Job-like righteous indignation, the supernaturalist rabbi will brush aside the theodicy problem with a facile comment on "hidden" or "unknowable" good. I have even heard this kind of answer offered to people who have experienced what Euripides called the greatest grief that can befall a person—to see one's child dead.[3]

Clearly, from a naturalistic perspective, the notion that God, who, like the Lord High Executioner in the *Mikado*, has a list of people to be dispatched (in a manner fitting their misdeeds) is hard to accept and, almost certainly false. It is, in short, a superstition, a belief in a causal connection between two things that have no causal connection. After decades of reflection, I conclude that the single most wrong-headed idea in our religion is that people suffer and die as divine punishment. Even to suggest it at a time of pain and loss is not only false, but cruel.

El Male Rahamim—אל מלא רחמים

El Male Rahamim, much more than the Mourners' *Kaddish*, is the essential Jewish prayer for the dead. While the Mourners' *Kaddish* is recited at every service, the *El Male Rahamim* is heard only at funeral and *shiva* services. But does a naturalist Jew find God to be full of compassion, as the prayer indicates?

Only an anthropomorphic God could be merciful or compassionate. Granted, when a person has suffered greatly and has no chance of recovery (*goses*)[4] it sometimes seems that death is a merciful gift. But this is a rationalization. A truly merciful God would have responded to all those *Misheberah* entreaties (the prayer for the blessing/healing of the sick) for a complete healing (*refuah shlema*), or at least complete enough to return to meaningful life.

A rabbi colleague once told me that the hardest conversation he had ever experienced was with a couple losing their young daughter to leukemia. Why, they wanted to know, did God allow this? I pointed out, however, that there was probably no man or woman on earth who could have

3. Euripides, *Suppliant Women*, verse 1120.
4. b. Git. 28a.

saved their child! Why, they might have asked, does an omnipotent and merciful god allow a small child to die face down in a shallow wading pool, something any present human being could have prevented?

We might also wonder why the granting of eternal rest or peace requires compassion or mercy. This suggests that all our deceased are undeserving of eternal rest and require divine intervention (or grace) to pardon their unworthiness. This could be viewed as a less egregious version of the notion that the deceased soul stays in a heavenly waiting room until his or her son has logged a year's worth of *kaddish* prayers.

Absent the reference to merciful intervention, the prayer is a rush of beautiful kabbalist imagery—a winged *Shehina* (the female essence of God), the pleasure of *Gan Eden* (the Garden of Eden, or Paradise). In some versions, there is a suggestion that charitable donations in the deceased's name will smooth the way to paradise, but this is a small, innocent superstition at worst. The theme of the prayer is rest, an echo of the Sabbath, and a less stark word that silence or oblivion. Shakespeare's Prospero says "our little life is rounded with a sleep."[5] And, because each of us has experienced rest and dreamless sleep, we are less afraid of what happens when our life ends.

To alleviate these concerns, one need only remove the opening words and begin the prayer with *Hamtzeh menuhah*—המצא מנוחה—May there be a perfect rest.

Adonay Natan, v'Adonay Lakah—ה׳ נתן וה׳ לקח

God has Given, and God has Taken Away

Often, in Jewish funeral services, the leader will recite this verse from the Book of Job, "God has given, God has taken away."[6] To those who hold a non-supernatural view of God, this sentence is superbly clear and inescapably true. God, as nature, initiates every life and enacts every death—but without any sense of reward, punishment, or divine purpose. Is this concept of God consistent with the meaning of this verse in its biblical context?

The portion of the Hebrew Bible that most sounds like a story from Greek mythology is Job. Although God is named YHVH, the God in this book is one of several heavenly beings including, most important, Satan the doubter. In the Greek world, human beings exist for the amusement of

5. Shakespeare, *Tempest*, Act IV, Scene 1.
6. Job 1:21.

the gods. They play tricks on them, engage them in combat, have sex with them, and, from time to time, place wagers on the outcomes of tasks they have contrived for them. The Greek gods may kill whatever human they want without invoking sacred laws, they may be merciful or not depending on their mood, and, as in Job, they will not be accountable for their actions. Zeus was not a righteous judge.

The *Adonay Natan* remark is uttered at a dramatic moment in the Job narrative. Several escaped messengers tell Job that his children were murdered by marauders and other disasters have destroyed his house, property, and all his wealth. These atrocities have been arranged by God to test Job's fidelity—and to win a wager with the Satan. Job's response, though, is what we might nowadays call philosophical: stuff happens!

Neither Job nor his children deserved any of this terror. Further, as God and Satan up the ante with more and more privations and inducements, Job remains philosophical until, at last, he breaks down and demands justice from God. And Job's God dismisses his demand with the back of his hand.

Ironically, although the God of Job is quite personal and psychologically motivated, there is nothing moral, ethical, righteous, merciful, or comforting in his attitude toward humankind. In this he is more like Nature, which is driven by its own inevitability and is indifferent to our lifespan.

Note the similarity in Spinoza's famous discussion of God:

> "By . . . God, I mean the fixed and unchangeable order of nature or the chain of natural events: for I have said before and shown elsewhere that the universal laws of nature, according to which all things exist and are determined, are only another name for the eternal decrees of God, which always involve eternal truth and necessity."[7]
>
> "We may thus clearly understand how far astray from a true estimate of virtue are those who expect to be decorated by God with high rewards for their virtue. . ."[8]

Adonay Natan, v'Adonay Lakah strikes me as an apt replacement for the *Dayan HaEmet*—Righteous Judge blessing. It is true and does not imply hurtful supernatural judgment.

---

7. Benedict Spinoza, *A Theological-Political Treatise*, III:13.
8. Benedict Spinoza, *Ethics*, II:49.

Kaddish—קדיש

The Mourners' *Kaddish*, that poetic admixture of Hebrew and Aramaic, is among our most familiar prayers. Spoken with earnest determination or through sobs of memory, we hear it often, and some of us every day, more than once.

It is a prayer of pure, outsized praise, with no petition and no demand for explanation or justification. And it has attained such an intensity of death-weighted feeling in our minds that we hardly care about the actual meaning of the words—which are rarely read in translation.

Although most who speak the prayer imagine a supernatural God, and many of those imagine that the saying of the prayer will influence the disposition of that God toward the deceased, there is nothing inherently supernatural in the text itself. The key to it are the end verses, the same verses that end the *Amidah*: *Oseh shalom bimromav*—Maker of Peace on High.

Shalom, which has several meanings, clearly refers here to the harmony of the spheres, the natural engine that keeps the celestial bodies in their orbits. Knowing this, when I prepared the eulogy for my son, a musician whose last performance was playing *Oseh Shalom* at our *Simhat Torah* celebration, I translated the verses as:

> May the source of harmony in the heavens,
> Give harmony to those below,
> Throughout Israel and the world.

At many funeral services, we introduce the Mourners' *Kaddish* with reflective readings. These vary considerably in quality and often convey curious messages, like "death is a destination." No reading, indeed none of the many Psalms spoken at funerals, should suggest that there is any other afterlife than that which exists in memory.

And it is time, I think, to supplement the chanting of the *Kaddish* with a suitable English translation-interpretation, to make it more than a rote incantation, something that speaks to us in English as well. To illustrate, consider this creative translation by the poet Marge Piercy. It begins:

> Look around us, search above us, below, behind.
> We stand in a great web of being joined together.
> Let us praise, let us love the life we are lent.

And it ends:

> Peace that bears joy into the world,

peace that enables love, peace over Israel
everywhere, blessed and holy is peace, let's say amen.[9]

I also find especially moving the works of several of the greatest English poets, like Swinburne:

> From too much love of living,
> From hope and fear set free,
> We thank with brief thanksgiving
> Whatever gods may be...
> That even the weariest river
> Winds somewhere safe to sea.[10]

COMFORT

The allure of the supernatural is greatest when we are in the presence of dying and death. Faced with the searing loss of a person we love, even the most rational and skeptical of people may pray fervently for miraculous cures. And when the miracles do not come, they try to ease their pain with thoughts of a pleasant afterlife, even the possibility of an eventual heavenly reunion with the departed.

When they are in distress, these people are entitled to whatever thoughts give them peace, even though the thoughts may strike others as irrational or superstitious. The changes and additions suggested in this essay would allow a naturalistic Jew to speak all the prayers in the funeral liturgy without embracing supernatural ideas. And these changes would probably go mostly unnoticed to those in mourning.

When there is a conflict, however, and a risk that the revised liturgy might disturb those who have lost someone they loved, the resolution should always be to set aside rationalism for a moment and give comfort to the mourners in Zion.

———————

Edmond H. Weiss, Ph.D., is a Professor Emeritus at Fordham University. Currently, he develops courses and seminars for adult Jewish education.

9. Piercy, *Blessing the Day*, 138.
10. Swinburne, *The Garden of Proserpine*, 747.

PART IV

LEARNING GUIDE

Questions, Dialogues, and Practica

—Rabbi Richard Agler

ON A BELIEVABLE GOD

If God is not, in significant measure, as he (sic) is described in Scripture, describe a God that is more believable for you.

If God is neither supernatural nor a miracle worker nor mythical, again as described in Scripture, how might God still be worthy of our service, devotion, and loyalty?

How does God reward the faithful and righteous and punish those who do evil? How does God *not* reward the faithful and righteous and punish those who do evil? Neither of these is meant to be a simple question. Contemplate, write, discuss.

A familiar view is that God is all-powerful, all-knowing, and all-good. Another is that God is all-powerful, all-caring, and all-just. Can God be all of these, both of these, each of these, or just some of these? Base your answers on either your own personal experience or on history as we know it.

The authors of this book present God in many different ways. Among them are:

- an Ordering Mind, Power, and Energy
- Law and Spirit
- the Power that Makes for Salvation

- the Laws of Science and the Principles of Morality
- the Creative Spiritual Seed of the Universe
- an expression of the Laws of Nature
- the All-Present, Ever-Present Now

Develop a God-understanding that resonates more fully with you. Take your time.

Maimonides wrote that evil is caused by nature, by other human beings, or is self-inflicted. (*Guide for the Perplexed*, 3:12) Interestingly, God is absent from his formulation. Can the same case be made for goodness, i.e., that it is either caused by nature, by other human beings, or is self-generated? And might God be part of this formulation?

Rabbi Harold Schulweis taught that God is best understood without resorting to nouns, as they inevitably fall short in attempting to capture God's essence. Verbs often do better. He described what he called Predicate Theology, where it is the "divinity of qualities," as opposed to the "qualities of divinity," that bring us closer to God-understanding. Explore this idea by creating sentences in which a divine attribute is part of the predicate.

Jewish faith has been described herein as Reverent Agnosticism. Explore and discuss what makes this an intriguing and challenging formulation.

At its essence, monotheistic faith holds that the universe is ordered design, not random chaos. Yet much that we observe seems chaotic and purposeless. Is it possible for us to reconcile these two perceptions? Can they both be true?

How can understanding God in non-personal terms, e.g., as Energy, Being, Conscious Force, Law, Spirit, etc., make faith more real? How does it make it more complex?

Talk, or write, about your own search for God. What have you discovered? What have you experienced? What mysteries remain? What might your next spiritual step(s) be?

ON BELIEVABLE WORDS

We appreciate that the Torah and other sacred Scriptures are products of their times. They contain much that is eternal, but also much that no longer aligns with our moral, scientific, or spiritual-religious understanding. Given this, how can we best incorporate venerable sacred texts into our lives?

God is often portrayed in Jewish sacred works as a Guardian-Protector, or *Shomer*—שומר. How is this, and how isn't this, a fitting description for God's relationship with the people Israel?

How can the Jewish tradition of interpreting scripture creatively and non-literally be a path to greater faith and belief? In what ways might even this technique be limited?

How can perceiving occurrences as miraculous, even when there is a natural explanation for them, facilitate our spiritual journeys?

Supernatural tales are pervasive throughout most religious traditions, including ours. Should we understand them:

- As a literal description of God's powers?
- As expressions of the ancient religious imagination?
- As a relief from the pain of everyday reality?
- As a reminder to appreciate the miraculous in our own lives?
- In some combination of the above—or in some other way?

Describe, discuss, compose, contemplate.

God is often portrayed in Scripture, as Maimonides teaches, in clearly metaphorical terms, e.g., King, Judge, Father, Warrior, etc. What metaphors might we use that would point us to a more believable God?

Who, or what, commands you? What is the source from which your personal moral imperative and ritual practices, whatever they may be, derive? Is it the traditional God of Scripture or something else? Describe that Source/source.

"*Ehyeh Asher Ehyeh*—אהיה אשר אהיה—I will be what I will be" (Exod 3:14) is the Name of God revealed to Moses at the burning bush. Yet this Name *almost* never appears in the traditional liturgy. (Extra credit if you know where!) Write a prayer that incorporates the Name *Ehyeh Asher Ehyeh*.

If God, in the traditional sense, neither hears our prayers nor answers them, what should prayer be? And how should we pray?

Are there things that God cannot reasonably be expected to do? Can praying to God actually free our captives, heal our sick, keep us from harm, bring peace where there is strife, etc.? If our prayers do not have the potential to change God's mind or to direct God's attention towards our specific needs, how might the liturgy be reframed to make such prayers more efficacious? Start by rewriting a problematic prayer.

Review the *siddur*—prayerbook that you use, or have at hand, closely. Identify traditional prayers that make sense to you. Also, note those that sound like they are addressed to a God in whom the ancients believed but by your lights, is not sufficiently real. Look for prayers that might be considered *tefilot shav*—empty, vain, or futile. Identify prayers that might be considered superstitious. How might these might be reworded to express more fitting sentiments or aspirations? Are there some that it might be better to remove from the formal liturgy altogether?

The Greek philosopher Epicurus offered, "Is God willing to prevent evil, but not able? Then he is not omnipotent. Is he able but not willing? Then he is malevolent. Is he both able and willing? Then from whence comes evil? Is he neither able nor willing? Then why call him God?" A corollary posits that either God wants to intervene but is not able to, or God is able to intervene and does not want to. Discuss the issue of believing in and addressing prayers to an intervening God.

The Hebrew verb "to pray—להתפלל—*l'hitpalel*," is reflexive. How might this guide us to a possible approach to prayer?

When we sincerely pray for something and it does not come to be, how does that impact our relationship with God? How does it impact our overall religious and spiritual life?

Identify some of the prayers that are set to music in your congregation. Which of them genuinely reflect your beliefs? Are there some that don't? What might be done about this?

Create a religious experience using only *Shabbat* candles, a small amount of *kiddush* wine, the people in the room, and their thoughts. Reflect on what made it meaningful.

Major project: Fashion a Jewish prayer service, or a portion of one, from scratch. It can be for waking up in the morning, retiring at night, before or after eating, for a *Shabbat*, holiday, or any other occasion. Which prayers speak believably to you? Include those. Which ones are problematic for one reason or another? Can they be reworked or reworded to make them acceptable? If so, do that. If not, set them aside for the moment. Endeavor to create prayers that are coherent, joyful, and thankful and that deepen our spiritual awareness.

ON BELIEVABLE HOLINESS

In our day, scientific knowledge is often privileged, and rightly so. Given this, how can religious faith best help us come to terms with the world of knowledge around us?

What should be the place for God in each of the following life cycle moments and ceremonies?:

- *Brit milah, Brit banot*, baby namings, and other rituals for welcoming newborns
- *Bar/Bat Mitzvah*
- *Kabbalat Torah*—Confirmation
- *Huppa v'Kiddushin*—Weddings
- *Gerut*—Conversion
- *Gittin*—Divorce
- Death—Funeral, *shiva, sheloshim, yahrzeit*

How should we order the concepts of Believing, Belonging, and Behaving as they apply to Jewish life? Which do you think should have priority? Which comes second, and which third?

What parts of Jewish faith should we be most intent on passing to the next generation? In a world that is so often divided and divisive, what parts of that message can help unite all of God's children?

How might it be possible to be an intellectually skeptical and a practicing, faithful Jew simultaneously?

Take a look at the Jewish holiday calendar. Consider the themes, messages, and rituals connected to each day. In which of them do you find God's traditional role more believable? In which ones is it less so? How might you modify your observance of the days to align them better with your understanding?

It is a core Jewish teaching to love God. (Deut 6:5) Is it possible to love a God who is non-personal? (Hint: the Hebrew word for love—אהבה, can also be understood as "serve.")

Rabbi Rami Schwartzer suggests that a way to approach God, and perhaps to feel God's Presence, "is to do nothing, to simply—stop. Stop trying, stop thinking, stop doing, stop achieving, and just be. Notice. Listen to what it sounds like for the breath to move in and out of your own nose. That's it—don't write about it, don't think about it, don't move any appendage or adjust your posture. Just stop, until another process in the body demands your attention and action with true urgency: hunger, thirst, expulsion, exhaustion. With those exceptions, just do nothing. This puts us in touch with the basic life functions, which of course puts us in touch with the source of those functions and reminds us what we are, what's important, and that everything else—everything—is ancillary. It is easy to describe—and extremely hard to do. But that's where we find God." Try it.

What do you think/believe happens to us after we die? How does your answer impact how we should live?

Science tells us that matter and energy are equivalent. And while they can take on new forms, they cannot be destroyed. With this in mind, contemplate what shapes or forms life after death might take.

Baruh Dayyan HaEmet—Blessed is the True Judge, *El Male Rahamim*—God filled with Compassion, *Adonai Natan, v'Adonai Lakah*—God gives and God takes away, and the *Kaddish* prayer are all familiar from the Jewish funeral liturgy. Which of these prayers do you find comforting? Do you find any of them disturbing? Why or why not?

If you've reached this point, congratulations! Since these are questions that can be pondered for many years, if not a lifetime, take a break, go back, and consider them again. Then repeat.

May your journey bring you ever-increasing understanding, more meaningful days, and greater peace. *Shalom.*

Acknowledgments

THIS VOLUME HAS BENEFITTED from the wisdom and counsel of many colleagues. We express our thanks for their contribution. They are:

Bob Alper; Elizabeth Bahar; Bruce Block; Andrea C; Hillel Cohn; Samuel Cohon; Neil Comess-Daniels; Ariel Edery; Micah Ellenson; Geoffrey Mitelman; Philip Graubart; Rachel Greengrass; Mark S. Kram; Howard Laibson; Anson Laytner; Mark Joel Mahler; Simeon H Maslin, *z"l*; Ralph Mecklenburger; Seymour Prystowsky; Sandy Eisenberg Sasso; Dennis Sasso; Rami Schwartzer; Jeffrey B. Stiffman, and Edmond H Weiss.

We would also like to thank our publisher Wipf and Stock, and especially, Assistant Managing Editor Emily Callihan, for her valuable advice and help. Thanks, too, to Mitch Feld for his thoughtful input.

Finally, in particular, we want to express our debt and gratitude to our spouses, Mindy Agler and Ines Sonsino, for their continual support during the creation of this book.

To all of the above, we extend our deepest appreciation. "May God reward your deeds." (Ruth 2:12)

Richard Agler and Rifat Sonsino

About the Editors

RABBI RICHARD DEAN AGLER is a native of New York City. He holds a Bachelor of Arts degree in Political Science from New York University (1973). From the Hebrew Union College–Jewish Institute of Religion, studying in Jerusalem and New York, he has received a Master of Arts in Hebrew Literature (1976), Rabbinic ordination (1978), and a Doctor of Divinity degree (2003).

Upon ordination, he served at the Stephen Wise Free Synagogue in Manhattan. He became the Founding Rabbi, now Rabbi Emeritus, of Congregation B'nai Israel in Boca Raton, Florida. During his twenty-seven-year tenure there, the congregation grew from four families in a living room to more than 1200 member families. He subsequently served as the Resident Scholar, now Scholar Emeritus, of the Keys Jewish Community Center/ Congregation Ohr Hayam in Tavernier, Florida.

Today, as Director of the Tali Fund, Inc., he supports the work of the Talia Agler Girls Shelter for trafficked, abused, and exploited girls in Nairobi, Kenya, and promotes awareness and registration for organ donation. He tours and lectures on this work, as well as on the themes and subjects of his first book, *The Tragedy Test: Making Sense of Life-Changing Loss* (2018).

He has been married since 1976 to the former Mindy Steinberg of Augusta, Georgia. They currently reside near their children and grandchildren in Southern California.

RABBI RIFAT SONSINO IS the Rabbi Emeritus of Temple Beth Shalom in Needham, MA.

Born in Turkey, he received his law degree from the University of Istanbul (Faculty of Law, 1959), his rabbinic ordination from the Hebrew Union College-Jewish Institute of Religion (Cincinnati, 1966), and his Ph.D. from the University of Pennsylvania (Philadelphia, 1975) in the field of Bible and ancient Near Eastern Studies. In 1991 the Hebrew Union College-Jewish Institute of Religion bestowed upon him a D.D.

Before coming to Needham, Rabbi Sonsino served congregations in Buenos Aires, Philadelphia, and Chicago. After his retirement from Beth Shalom, he volunteered his services at Bet Shalom, a nascent Reform Jewish congregation in Barcelona, Spain, and other small synagogues in the Iberian Peninsula.

Rabbi Sonsino has authored numerous books and articles, including *Finding God* and *What Happens After I Die?* (both with Daniel Syme), *The Many Faces of God, Modern Judaism, And God Spoke These Words* (commentary of the 10 Commandments), and *Did Moses Really Have Horns?* He was the editor of the *CCAR Journal* from 1997–2001. Throughout his career, Rabbi Sonsino has chaired various committees, both regionally and nationally. His blog postings (SONSINO'S BLOG) are found at rsonsino. blogspot.com, with over half a million viewers. In the past, Rabbi Sonsino taught at Boston College and at Framingham State University and lectured in many parts of the country and around the world.

Rabbi and Mrs. Sonsino now live at the Willows in Westborough, MA.

Bibliography

American Association for the Advancement of Science. "Perceptions: Science and Religious Communities." 2015. https://www.aaas.org/sites/default/files/content_files/PerceptionsFinalReport.pdf, 8–9.

Borowitz, Eugene B. *Liberal Judaism*. New York: Union of American Hebrew Congregations, 1984.

Buber, Martin. *Tales of the Hasidim: Early Masters*. New York: Schocken, 1975.

Burger, Ariel. *Witness: Lessons from Elie Wiesel's Classroom*. Boston: Mariner Books, Houghton Mifflin Harcourt, 2018.

Central Conference of American Rabbis. *Rabbi's Manual, Revised*. New York: CCAR, 1961.

———. *Union Prayer Book*. New York: CCAR, 1940.

Cohen, Arthur A. *The Tremendum: A Theological Interpretation of the Holocaust*. New York: Continuum, 1993.

Cordovero, Moses. *Shi'ur Qomah*, translated by Daniel Matt in *The Essential Kabbalah*. New York: Harper Collins, 2010.

Dennett, Daniel C. *Darwin's Dangerous Idea: Evolution and the Meanings of Life*. New York: Simon and Schuster, 1995.

Deutsch, Gotthard, et al. *Purims, Special*. The Jewish Encyclopedia, 1906. https://jewishencyclopedia.com/articles/12450-purims-special

Edery, Ariel, ed. *Siddur: Shabbat Morning*. Raleigh: Beth Shalom, 2009. https://images.shulcloud.com/13437/uploads/Religious-School-Files/Morning-Siddur-2009.pdf, 46.

Eisenstein, Ira. *Judaism Under Freedom*. New York: Reconstructionist, 1956.

———. *Reconstructing Judaism: An Autobiography*. New York: Reconstructionist, 1986.

———. *What We Mean By Religion*. New York: Reconstructionist, 1964.

Freehof, Solomon B. *Spoken and Heard Sermon and Address*. Wheeling, WV: Boyd, 1972.

Friedman, Richard Elliott. *The Hidden Face of God*. New York: Harper Collins, 1995.

Frishman, Elyse D., ed. *Mishkan T'filah: A Reform Siddur*. New York: Central Conference of American Rabbis, 2007.

Fromm, Eric. *Psychoanalysis and Religion*. New Haven: Yale University Press, 1958.

Gittelsohn, Roland B. *A Jewish View of God*. New York: Judaism Pamphlet Series, B'nai B'rith Youth Organization, 1965.

———. *Wings of the Morning*. New York: Union of American Hebrew Congregations, 1969.

Bibliography

Goldberg, Edwin, et al., eds. *Mishkan HaNefesh: Yom Kippur Machzor for the Days of Awe*, New York: Central Conference of American Rabbis, 2015.

Goldman, Steven L. "Science Wars: What Scientists Know and How They Know It." 2012. https://www.thegreatcourses.com/courses/science-wars-what-scientists-know-and-how-they-know-it.

Greenberg, Sidney. *A Treasury of Comfort*. Woodland Hills, CA: Wilshire, 1978.

Hawking, Stephen. *Brief Answers to the Big Questions*. New York: Bantam, 2018.

Heschel, Abraham J. and Heschel, Susannah, ed. *Abraham Joshua Heschel: Essential Writings*. Maryknoll, NY: Orbis, 2011.

Heschel, Abraham J. *God in Search of Man*. Philadelphia: Jewish Publication Society, 1962.

———. *Man's Quest for God*. New York: Charles Scribners, 1954.

———. *Who Is Man?* Stanford, CA: Stanford University Press, 1965.

Hume, David. *Dialogue Concerning Natural Religion*. Cambridge: Hackett, 1998.

Jacob, Walter., ed. *American Reform Responsa*. New York, Central Conference of American Rabbis, 1983.

Jacobs, Joseph, et al. *Kol Nidre*. The Jewish Encyclopedia, 1906. https://jewishencyclopedia.com/articles/9443-kol-nidre.

Kaplan, Mordecai. *Not So Random Thoughts*. New York: Reconstructionist, 1966.

———. *Questions Jews Ask*. New York: Reconstructionist, 1956.

Kaplan, Mordecai, et al. *The Faith of America; Readings, Songs, and Prayers for the Celebration of American Holidays*. New York: Reconstructionist, 1963.

Knobel, Peter S., ed. *Gates of the Seasons*. New York: Central Conference of American Rabbis, 1983.

Kripke, Dorothy. *Let's Talk About Being Jewish*. New York: Ktav, 1981.

Kushner, Lawrence. *Eyes Remade for Wonder*. Woodstock, VT: LongHill Partners, 1998.

Maimonides, Moses. *Guide to the Perplexed*. Translated by M. Friedlaender - Edited and Compiled by Paul A. Böer, Sr., Edmond, OK: Veritatis Splendor, Kindle edition. 2013.

Matt, Daniel C. *God and the Big Bang*. Woodstock, VT: Jewish Lights Publishing, 1996.

Mecklenburger, Ralph. *Our Religious Brains*. Woodstock, VT: Jewish Lights and Skylight Paths, 2012.

———. *Why Call It God? Theology for the Age of Science*. Eugene, OR: Wipf & Stock, 2020.

Mitelman, Geoffrey. *Science and Truth, in These Truths We Hold*. Cincinnati: HUC Press, Forthcoming.

Mother Teresa of Calcutta. *In the Heart of the World: Thoughts, Stories and Prayers*. Canada: ReadHowYouWant.com, Limited, 2010.

Nelson, David W. *Judaism, Physics and God*. Woodstock, VT: Jewish Lights, 2005.

Overbye, Dennis. *New York Times*, April 8, 2021.

Pew Research Center. "Belief in God," 2014. http://www.pewforum.org/religious-landscape-study/belief-in-god.

———. "Jewish American Beliefs," 2013. https://www.pewforum.org/2013/10/01/jewish-american-beliefs-attitudes-culture-survey/.

———. "Jewish Americans in 2020," 2021. https://www.pewforum.org/2021/05/11/jewish-americans-in-2020/.

Piercy, Marge. *The Art of Blessing the Day*. New York: Knopf, 1998.

Plaut, W. Gunther. *Rabbi's Manual—Maaglei Tzedek*. New York: Central Conference of American Rabbis, 1988

———. *The Rise of Reform Judaism*. New York: World Union for Progressive Judaism, 1963.

Polydox Institute. Alvin J. Reines. "The Term Polydoxy." https://polydoxy.org/the-term-polydoxy/.

———. "Questions and Answers." https://polydoxy.org/questions-answers/.

———. "Wedding Ceremony." https://polydoxy.org/wp-content/uploads/2015/11/WeddingCer_8B.pdf.

Pritchard, James B. ed. *Ancient Near Eastern Texts*. Princeton, NJ: Princeton University Press, 1969.

Pullman, Philip, and Simon Mason. *The Origin of the Universe, Dæmon Voices: On Stories and Storytelling*. New York: Knopf, 2018.

Reines, Alvin J. *Polydoxy*. Lanham, MD: Prometheus, 1987.

———. *Shabbath As a State of Being*. New York: CCAR Journal, January 1967.

Sagan, Carl. *The Demon-Haunted World: Science as a Candle in the Dark*. New York: Ballantine, 2011.

Sasso, Eisenberg Sandy. *For Heaven's Sake*. Illustrated by K. K. Finney. Woodstock, VT: Jewish Lights, 1999.

———. *God's Paintbrush*. Illustrated by A. Compton. Woodstock, VT: Jewish Lights, 1992.

———. *In God's Name*. Illustrated by P. Stone. Woodstock, VT: Jewish Lights, 1994.

Schulweis, Harold. *For Those Who Can't Believe: Overcoming the Obstacles to Faith*. New York: HarperCollins, 1995.

Silverman, William. *Religion for Skeptics*. New York: Jonathan David, 1967

Solomon, Dan. *A Jewish Perspective on Religious Naturalism, Routledge Handbook of Religious Naturalism*. Edited by Donald A. Crosby and Jerome Stone. London: Routledge, 2018.

Soloveitchik, Joseph. *The Lonely Man of Faith*. Tradition Magazine, Summer 1965, New York: Rabbinical Council of America, 1965.

Sommer, Benjamin. *Revelation & Authority: Sinai in Jewish Scripture and Tradition*. New Haven: Yale University Press, 2015.

Sonsino, Rifat, and Daniel Syme, eds. *What Happens After I Die*. New York: Union of American Hebrew Congregations, 1990.

Stern, Chaim, ed. *Gates of Prayer*. New York: Central Conference of American Rabbis, 1975.

———. *Gates of Repentance*. New York: Central Conference of American Rabbis, 1999.

Swinburne, Algernon Charles. "The Garden of Proserpine." In *The New Oxford Book of English Verse: 1250–1950*, edited by Helen Gardner. Oxford: Oxford University Press, 1972.

Tanakh. Philadelphia: Jewish Publication Society, 1985.

Tunstall, Elizabeth Dori. "How Maya Angelou Made Me Feel." *The Conversation*, May 29, 2014. https://theconversation.com/how-maya-angelou-made-me-feel-27328.

Wiesel, Elie. *Sages and Dreamers*. New York: Summit Books, 1991.

Wurzburger, Walter. *Ethics of Responsibility*. Philadelphia: Jewish Publication Society, 1994.

———. *Theological and Philosophical Responses to the Holocaust: Issues in Teaching the Holocaust: A Guide*. New York: Yeshiva University Press, 1981.

CPSIA information can be obtained
at www.ICGtesting.com
Printed in the USA
JSHW040758290522
26077JS00001B/11